ABGAD

Modern Standard Arabic
For
English Speakers

اللغة العربية الفصحى الحديثة للناطقين بالإنجليزية

First Year Arabic - Semesters 1 & 2
College level

ACTFL Proficiency Levels: Novice - Intermediate Low

DAHLIA DWEDAR, PhD

Thebes, LLC

Arizona

Sound, Script and More

THIRD EDITION, 2020

This book is printed on a paper suitable for recycling and made from fully managed and sustained forest sources.

Printed in the United States of America.

For free desk copies, quizzes & homeowrks packet contact the author @ Dr.DahliaDwedar@aol.com From a .EDU email.
All Audio Files are available on the YouTube Chanel: Arabic for English Speakers - College Levels

Thebes LLC, AZ

Table of Contents

Useful Maps

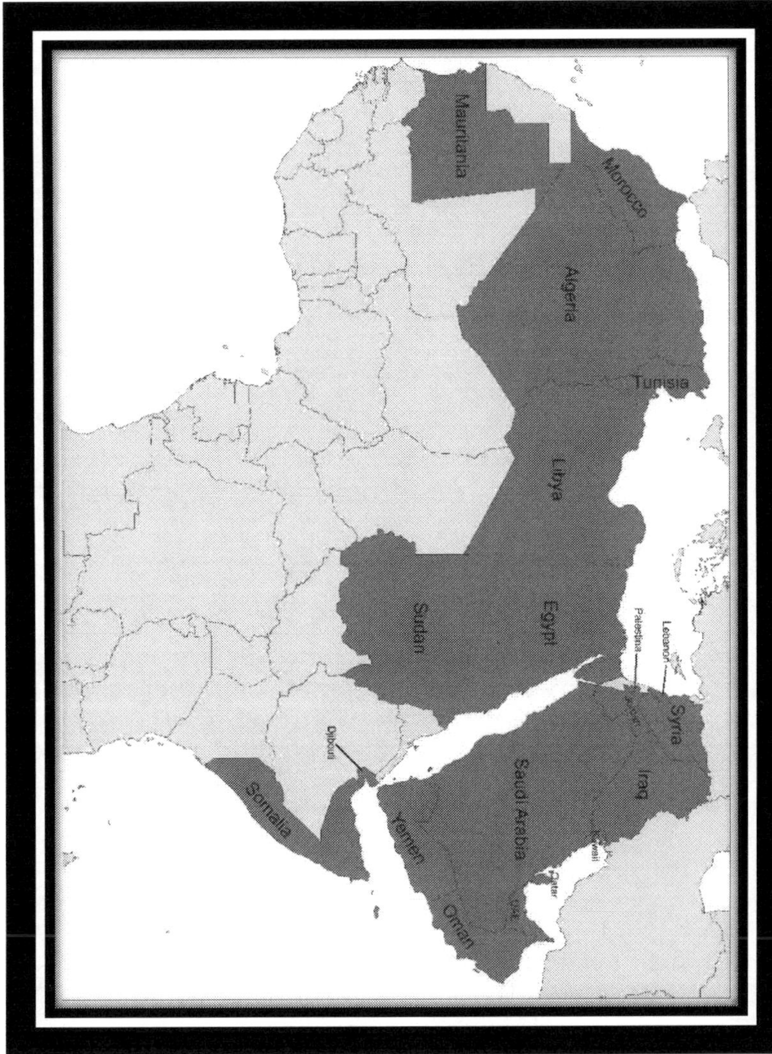

The countries where Standard Arabic is an official language. Some of them do have other official languages, the original languages of the natives.

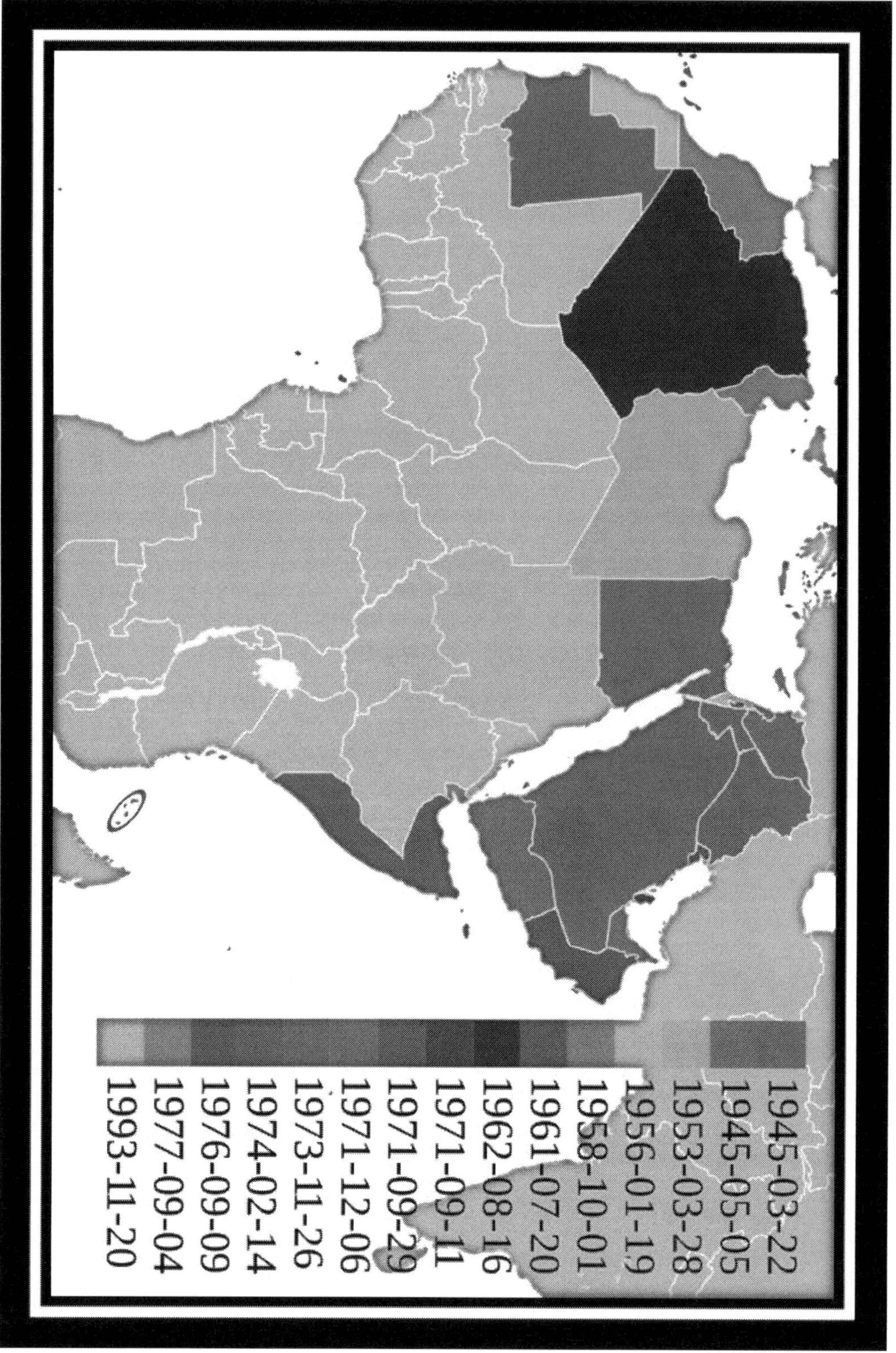
1945-03-22
1945-05-05
1953-03-28
1956-01-19
1958-10-01
1961-07-20
1962-08-16
1971-09-11
1971-09-29
1971-12-06
1973-11-26
1974-02-14
1976-09-09
1977-09-04
1993-11-20

Map showing the year each country has joined the Arab league

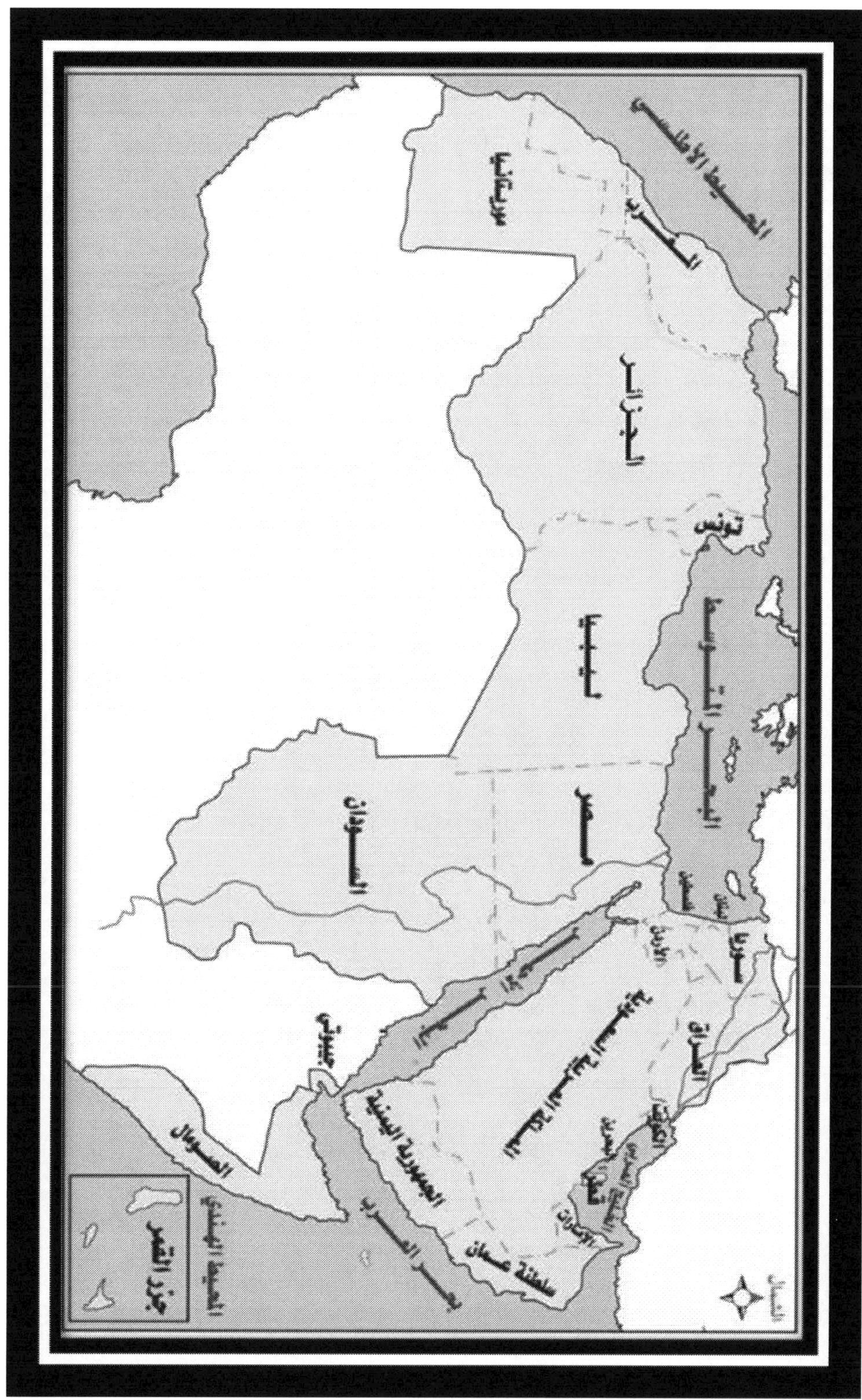

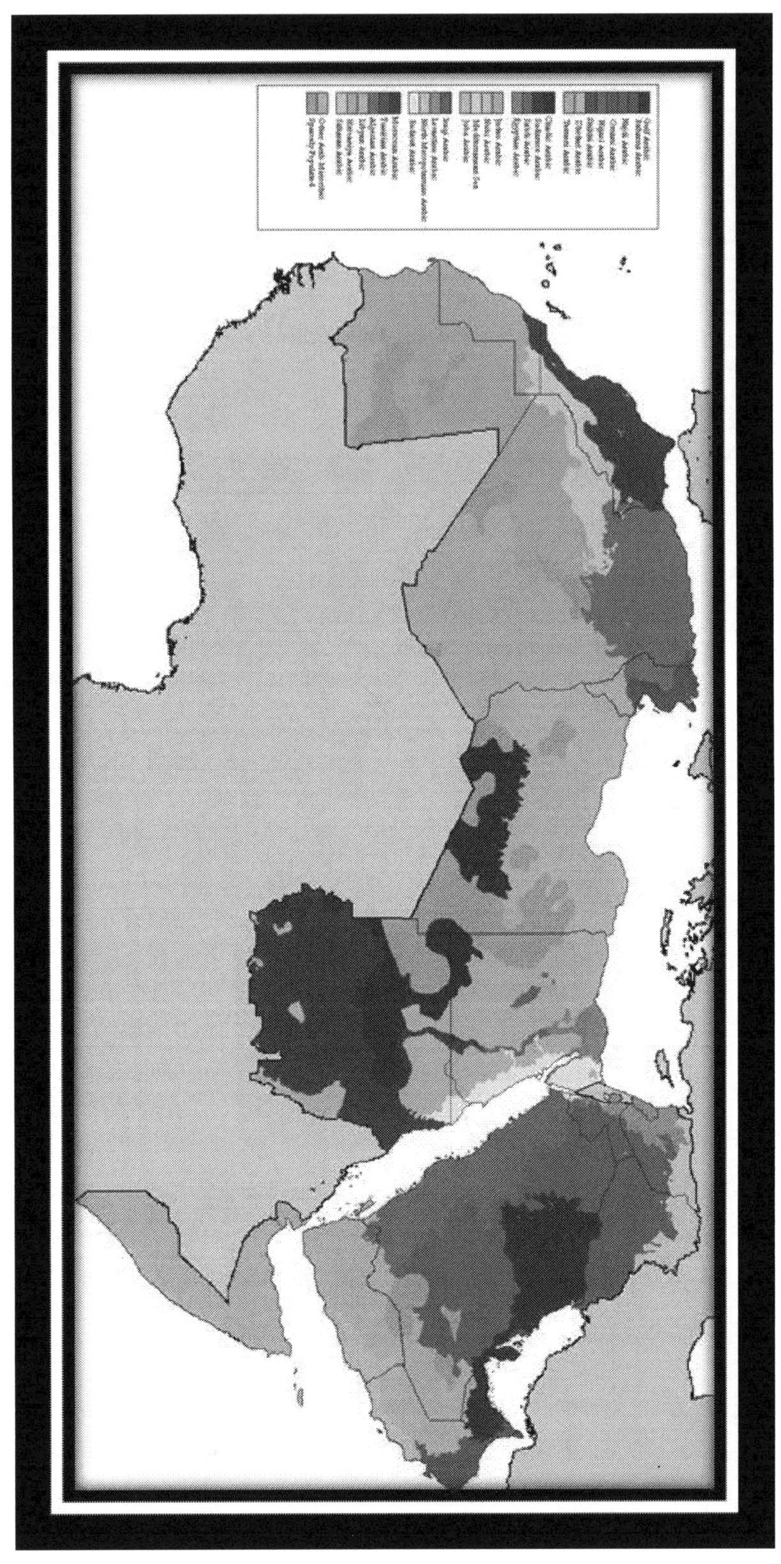

Map showing the different dialects in the region

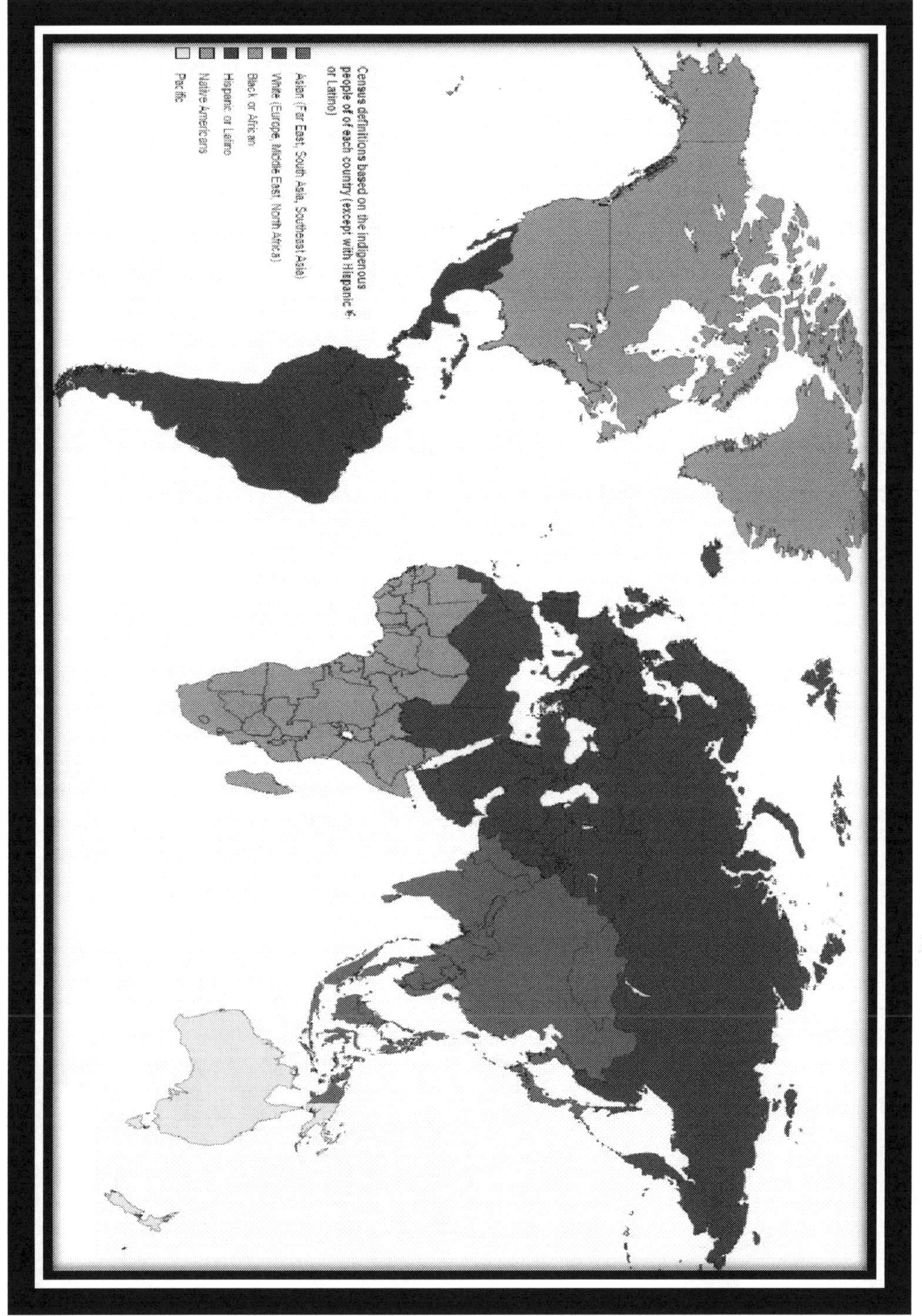
Census definitions based on the indigenous people of of each country (except with Hispanic & or Latino)
Asian (Far East, South Asia, Southeast Asia)
White (Europe, Middle East, North Africa)
Black or African
Hispanic or Latino
Native Americans
Pacific

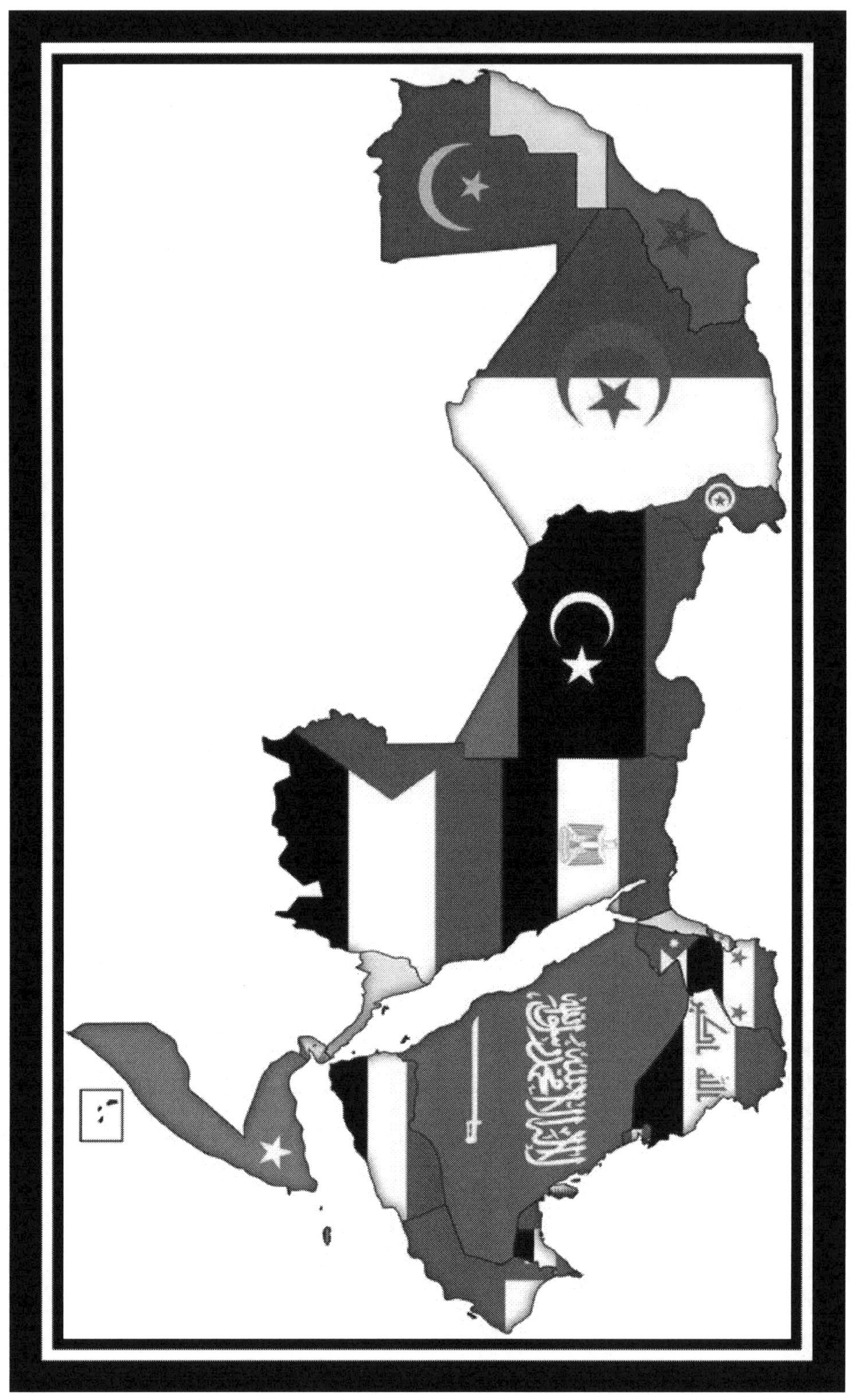

Map showing the flag of each Arab speaking countries

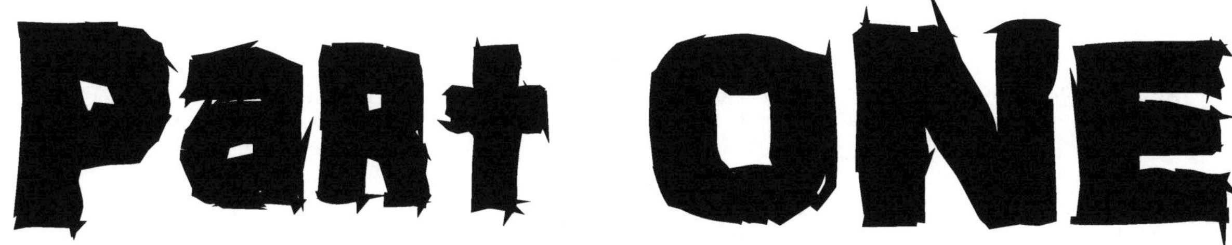

The Arabic Language

Arabic is classified as a Central Semitic language, and linguists widely agree that the language first emerged in the 1st to 4th centuries CE.

Arabic is the *lingua franca* of 22 countries of the Middle East and as a second language in 34 other countries.

Arabic is named after the Arabs, a term initially used to describe peoples living in the area bounded by Mesopotamia in the east and the Lebanon mountains in the west, in northwestern Arabia, and in the Sinai Peninsula.

Arabic is comprising 30 modern dialects, including its standard form, Modern Standard Arabic, which is derived from Classical Arabic and other languages.

During the Middle Ages, Literary Arabic was a major vehicle of culture in Europe, especially in science, mathematics and philosophy. As a result, many European languages have also borrowed many words from it.

Arabic influence, mainly in vocabulary, is seen mainly in Spanish and to a lesser extent Portuguese, and Catalan, owing to both the proximity of Christian European and Muslim Arab civilizations and 800 years of Arabic culture and language in the Iberian Peninsula, referred to in Arabic as *Al-Andalus*.

Sicilian has about 500 Arabic words as result of Sicily being progressively conquered by North Africans, from the mid-9th to mid-10th centuries. Many of these words relate to agriculture.

The Balkan languages, including Greek and Bulgarian, have also acquired a significant number of Arabic words through contact with Ottoman Turkish.

Classical Arabic is the liturgical language of 1.8 billion Muslims.

Modern Standard Arabic is one of **six** official languages of the United Nations.

Arabic is spoken by approximately 422 million speakers, which makes it the fifth most spoken language in the world, after English, Chinese Hindi, and Spanish.

According to the 2010 U.S. Census, there are *1,698,570* Arabic speaking Americans in the United States and *3,700,000* according to the Arab American Institute.

The largest subgroup is by far the **Lebanese** then the **Egyptian** then the **Syrian then** Palestinians, and **Jordanian**.

The Arabic Language Script

The Arabic writing system has some major characteristics that distinguish it from English:

- Arabic is written from right to left.
- No capital forms for the Arabic letters as in the Latin alphabet at the beginning of a sentence and with proper nouns.
- Few Arabic letters have multiple forms, depending on whether the letter is connected to a preceding or a following letter, or to both, or to neither. (ـه – ي)
- 6 letters of the Arabic Alphabet do not connect to letters that follow.
- No Silent letters escept in one case.
- Arabic the short vowels are normally not represented in writing like English, rather they are indicated by small diacritic marks placed above or below the consonant letters. There are 3 main short diacritic marks representing the short vowels.
- The Arabic language authentic printed text such as books, magazines, newspapers, street signs, is not vowel led. Therefore, Students will notice that, gradually the diacritic marks will be removed. Consequently, students are required to become accustomed to reading Arabic text without diacritic marks.
- Consonant sounds are represented in writing by letters, each letter represents a sound.
- Arabic requires a vowel in every syllable, unlike the English language which allows consonant clusters such as the /str/ in strength. The exception is cognates, or “loan” words, which may contain consonant clusters.

LESSON 1

Syria- Al Hamidya- Umayyad Mosque

Arabic Alphabet

The Arabic Alphabet with Equivalent Sound in English

	ث Thaa- thunder	ت Taa-T	ب Baa-B	ا Ailf - A
		خ Khaa- kh	ح Haa- h	ج Gim/jim- G/J
	ز Zain-Z	ر Ra-R	ذ Thal- the	د Dal-D
			ش Shin- Sh	س Sin- S
	ظ Thah- Th	ط Tah-T	ض Dad- D	ص Sad- S
			غ Ghayn	ع Ayn
			ق Qaf-Q	ف Faa- F
			ل Lam-L	ك Kaf-K
ي Yaa- Y	و Wao- W	هـ Haa-H	ن Noun-N	مـ Mim-M

Group 1

ث Thaa- thunder	ت Taa-T	ب Baa-B	ا Ailf - A
	خ Khaa- kh	ح Haa- h	ج Gim/jim- G/J
ز Zain-Z	ر Ra-R	ذ Thal- the	د Dal-D

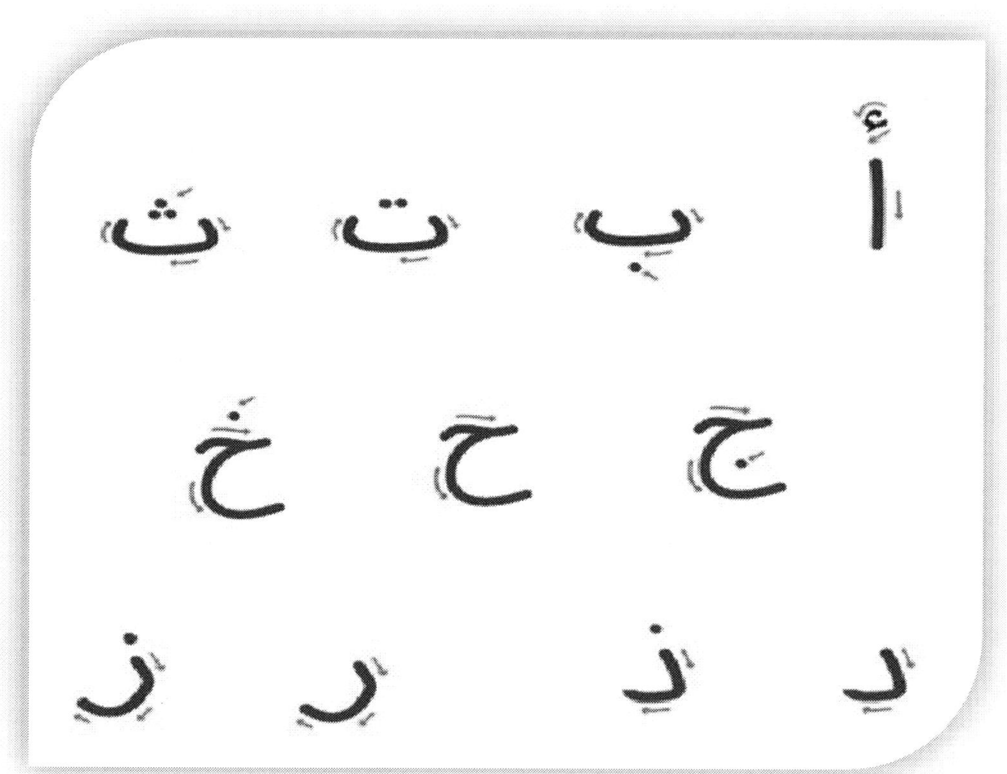

أ ب ت ث

ج ح خ

د ذ ر ز

أ ب ت ث

ج ح خ

د ذ ر ز

أ ب ت ث

ج ح خ

د ذ ر ز

أ ب ت ث

ج ح خ

د ذ ر ز

أ ب ت ث

ج ح خ

د ذ ر ز

أ ب ت ث

ج ح خ

د ذ ر ز

Group 2			
ش Shin- Sh		س Sin- S	
ظ **Thah- Th**	ط **Tah-T**	ض **Dad- D**	ص **Sad- S**

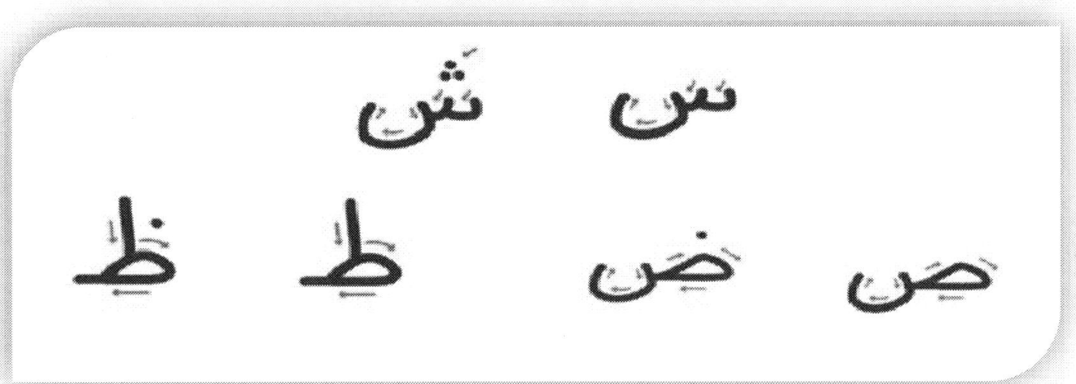

س ش ص ض ط ظ س ش ص ض ط ظ	س ش ص ض ط ظ س ش ص ض ط ظ

س ش
ص ض ط ظ
س ش
ص ض ط ظ

س ش
ص ض ط ظ
س ش
ص ض ط ظ

س ش
ص ض ط ظ
س ش
ص ض ط ظ

س ش
ص ض ط ظ
س ش
ص ض ط ظ

س ش
ص ض ط ظ
س ش
ص ض ط ظ

س ش
ص ض ط ظ
س ش
ص ض ط ظ

Group 3	
غ **Ghayn**	ع **Ayn**
ق **Qaf-Q**	ف **Faa- F**
ل **Lam-L**	ك **Kaf-K**

ع غ ع غ ع غ
ف ق ك ل

ع غ ع غ ع غ
ف ق ك ل

ع غ
ف ق ك ل

ع غ
ف ق ك ل

ع غ ع غ ع غ
ف ق ك ل

ع غ ع غ ع غ
ف ق ك ل

ع غ ع غ ع غ
ف ق ك ل

ع غ ع غ ع غ
ف ق ك ل

Group 4				
ي	و	هـ	ن	مـ
Yaa- Y	Wao- W	Haa-H	Noun-N	Mim-M

م م م ن ن ن هـ هـ و و ي ي ي	م ن ن ن هـ هـ و و ي ي ي

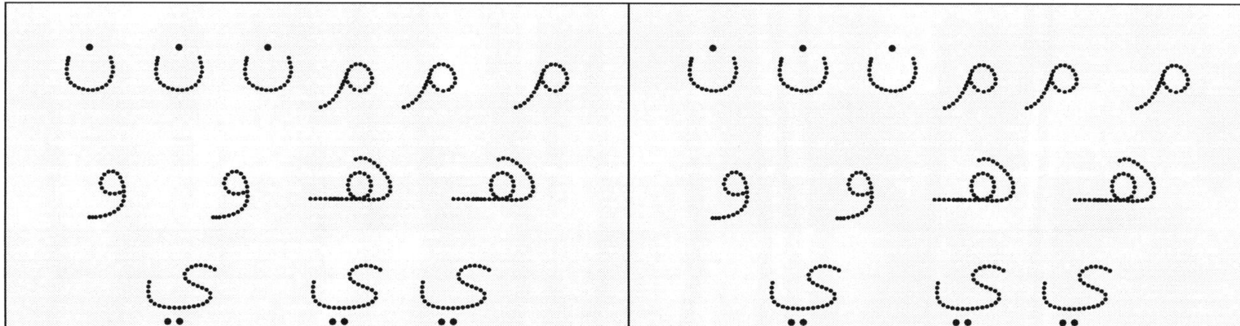

م م م ن ن ن
هـ هـ و و
ي ي ي

م م م ن ن ن
هـ هـ و و
ي ي ي

م م م ن ن ن
هـ هـ و و
ي ي ي

م م م ن ن ن
هـ هـ و و
ي ي ي

م م م ن ن ن
هـ هـ و و
ي ي ي

م م م ن ن ن
هـ هـ و و
ي ي ي

Letters that are similar in pronunciation	
د - ض	ت - ط
ذ - ز	ث - س
ذ - ظ	س - ص
ق - ك	

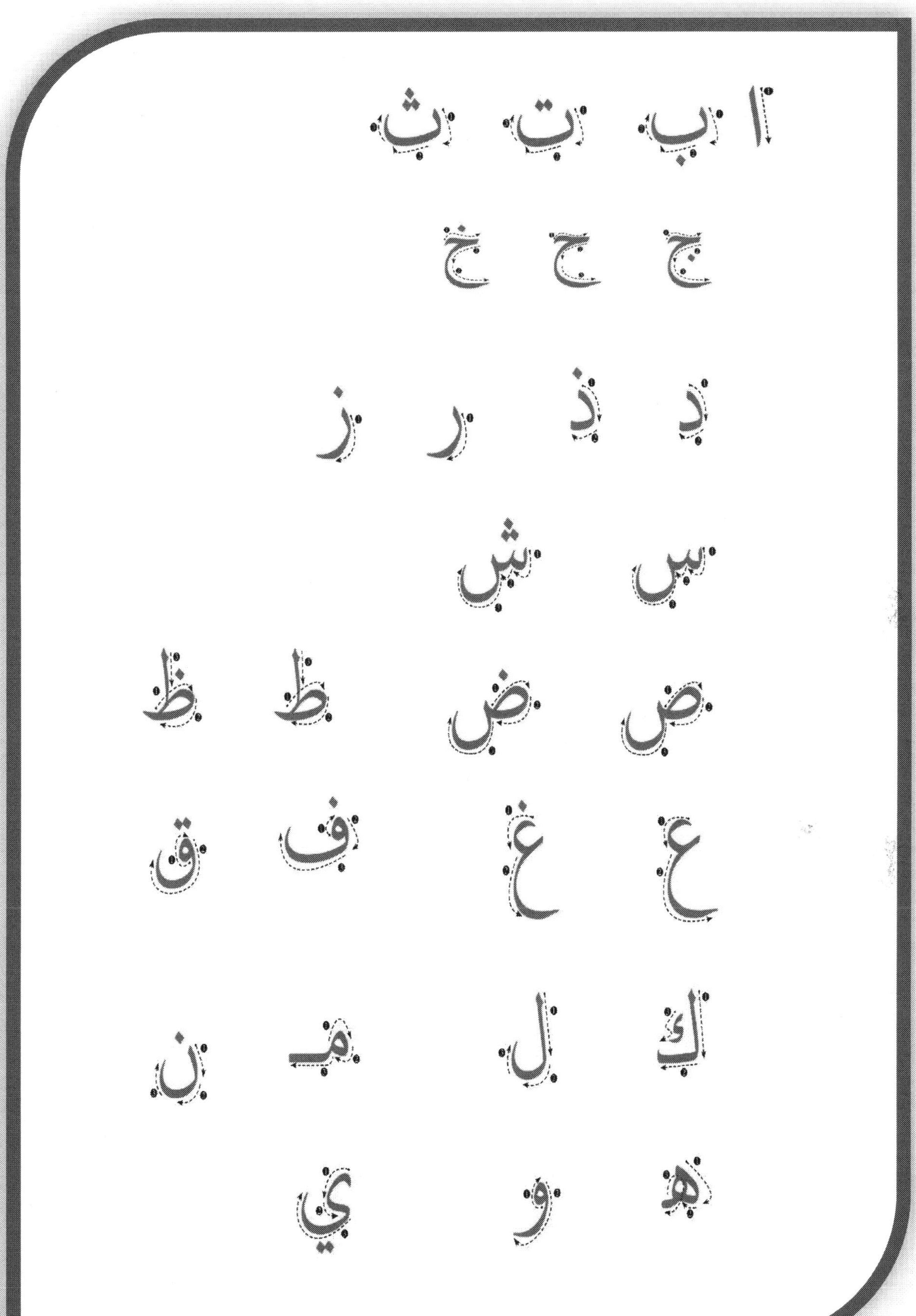

ا ب ت ث
ج ح خ
د ذ ر ز
س ش
ص ض ط ظ
ع غ ف ق
ك ل م ن
هـ و ي

أَ بِ تَ ثَ

جَ حَ خَ

دِ ذِ رِ زِ

سَ شَ

صِ ضَ طِ ظِ

عَ غَ فَ قِ

كَ لِ مـ نِ

هـ وَ يِ

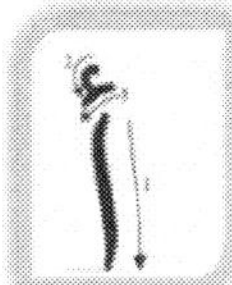

أ أ

ب ت ث ب ت ث ب ت ث ب ت ث ب ت ث ب ت ث

ج ح خ ج ح خ ج ح خ ج ح خ ج ح خ ج ح خ

د ذ د ذ د ذ د ذ د ذ د ذ د ذ د ذ د ذ د ذ د ذ

ز ر ز ر ز ر ز ر ز ر ز ر ز ر ز ر ز ر ز ر ز ر ز

س ش س ش س ش س ش س ش س ش

ص ض ص ض ص ض ص ض ص ض ص ض ص ض

ط ظ ط ظ ط ظ ط ظ ط ظ ط ظ ط ظ ط ظ ط ظ ط ظ ط

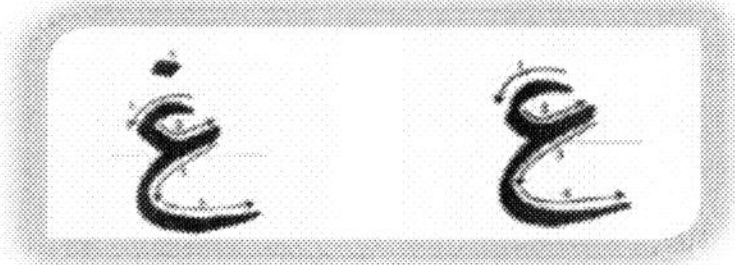

ع غ ع غ ع غ ع غ ع غ ع غ ع غ ع غ ع غ

ف ق ف ق ف ق ف ق ف ق ف ق ف ق ف ق ف ق

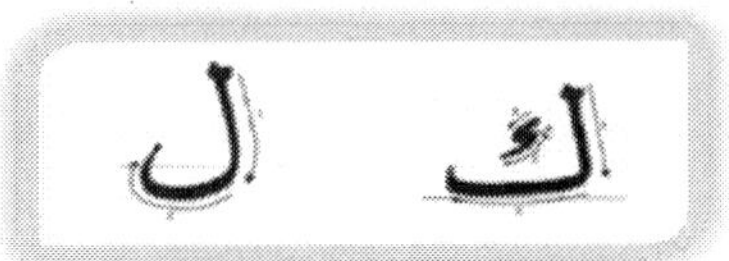

ك ل ك ل ك ل ك ل ك ل ك ل ك ك ل ك ل ك ل ك ل

م ن م ن م ن م ن م ن م ن م ن م ن م ن م ن م ن

هـ هـ هـ هـ هـ هـ هـ هـ هـ هـ هـ هـ هـ هـ هـ هـ

و ي و ي و ي و ي و ي و ي و ي و ي و ي و ي و ي

The Arabic Alphabet In Different Fonts

أ ب ت ث   ج ح خ   د ذ   ر ز

س ش   ص ض   ط ظ

ع غ   ف ق   ك ل

مـ ن   هـ و ي

_ _ _ _ _ _ _

أ ب ت ث   ج ح خ   د ذ   ر ز

س ش   ص ض   ط ظ

ع غ   ف ق   ك ل

مـ ن   هـ و ي

LESSON 2

Yemen - Sanaa

How to Connect the Arabic Alphabet letters

The 6 unsocial letters or Kicking letters		
These letters can only connect with other letters placed before them and not after, which means that if a letter is placed after them, that letter should take a form as if it was placed in the beginning of the word.		
ذ	د	أ
و	ز	ر

Final -Medial -Initial	Letter	Final –Medial- Initial	Letter
طـ ـطـ ـط	ط	ا ـا ـا	أ
ظـ ـظـ ـظ	ظ	بـ ـبـ ـب	ب
عـ ـعـ ـع	ع	تـ | ـتـ | ـت ـة ة	ت
غـ ـغـ ـغ	غ	ثـ ـثـ ـث	ث
فـ ـفـ ـف	ف	جـ ـجـ ـج	ج
قـ ـقـ ـق	ق	حـ ـحـ ـح	ح
كـ ـكـ ـك	ك	خـ ـخـ ـخ	خ
لـ ـلـ ـل	ل	د ـد ـد	د
مـ ـمـ ـم	م	ذ ـذ ـذ	ذ
نـ ـنـ ـن	ن	ر ـر ـر	ر
هـ | ـهـ | ـه ه	هـ	ز ـز ـز	ز
و ـو ـو	و	سـ ـسـ ـس	س
يـ ـيـ ـي	ي	شـ ـشـ ـش	ش
		صـ ـصـ ـص	ص
		ضـ ـضـ ـض	ض

With your teacher practice Connecting the following letters

We will start with the group letters: أ ب ت ث ج ح خ

Not all the following words are real words:

ث ا ب ت ← ثــابــت

ث ب ت

ث ب ا ت

ب ث ا ث

ب ت ا ت

خ ب ث ← خــبــث

ج ب ت

ج ب ح

ا ج ت ب ا

ب ت ا ح

ACTIVITY 1: Trace the Alphabet in joining positions

أ ـا

بـ تـ ثـ / ـبـت

جـ حـ خـ / ـجـ ـح

د ذ ر ز

أ ـا

بـ تـ ثـ / ـبـت

جـ حـ خـ / ـجـ ـح

د ذ ر ز

أ ـا

بـ تـ ثـ / ـبـت

جـ حـ خـ / ـجـ ـح

د ذ ر ز

أ ـا

بـ تـ ثـ / ـبـت

جـ حـ خـ / ـجـ ـح

د ذ ر ز

أ ـا

بـ تـ ثـ / ـبـت

جـ حـ خـ / ـجـ ـح

د ذ ر ز

أ ـا

بـ تـ ثـ / ـبـت

جـ حـ خـ / ـجـ ـح

د ذ ر ز

ACTIVITY 2: Trace the Alphabet in joining positions

أ ـا

بـ تـ ثـ / ـبـــت

جـ حـ خـ / ـجـ ـح

د ذ ر ز

أ ـا

بـ تـ ثـ / ـبـــت

جـ حـ خـ / ـجـ ـح

د ذ ر ز

أ ـا

بـ تـ ثـ / ـبـــت

جـ حـ خـ / ـجـ ـح

د ذ ر ز

أ ـا

بـ تـ ثـ / ـبـــت

جـ حـ خـ / ـجـ ـح

د ذ ر ز

أ ـا

بـ تـ ثـ / ـبـــت

جـ حـ خـ / ـجـ ـح

د ذ ر ز

أ ـا

بـ تـ ثـ / ـبـــت

جـ حـ خـ / ـجـ ـح

د ذ ر ز

ACTIVITY 3: Practice Connecting the following letters. We will add this the group of letters د ذ ر ز ز

Not all the following words are real words:

ا ب ت ز ⟵ ابــتــز

ب ت ر ا　　　ح ب ر

ت ا ر ا　　　ب ر ا د

ب ا ر د　　　ر ز ا ز

ز ا ر ا　　　ب د ا ر ا

ACTIVITY 4 : Trace the Alphabet in joining positions

أ ـا بـ تـ ثـ / ـبـ ـت جـ حـ خـ / ـجـ ـح د ذ ر ز سـ شـ / ـشـ ـس صـ ضـ / ـضـ ـص ط ظ / ـطـ ـط	أ ـا بـ تـ ثـ / ـبـ ـت جـ حـ خـ / ـجـ ـح د ذ ر ز سـ شـ / ـشـ ـس صـ ضـ / ـضـ ـص ط ظ / ـطـ ـط

أ ـا بـ تـ ثـ / ـبـ ـت جـ حـ خـ / ـجـ ـح د ذ ر ز سـ شـ / ـشـ ـس صـ ضـ / ـضـ ـص ط ظ / ـطـ ـط	أ ـا بـ تـ ثـ / ـبـ ـت جـ حـ خـ / ـجـ ـح د ذ ر ز سـ شـ / ـشـ ـس صـ ضـ / ـضـ ـص ط ظ / ـطـ ـط

ACTIVITY 5: Practice Connecting the following letters. We will add this the group of letters

س ش ص ض

ش ذ ر ا ت ← شـــذرات

س ر د ا ب

ش ب ت

ش ر ا ر

ر د

ض ر ب ا ← ضــربــا

ص د ر

ت ض ا د

ض ا ب ط

ض ر ر

ACTIVITY 6: Trace the Alphabet in joining positions

أ ا

بـ تـ ثـ / ـبـت

جـ حـ خـ / ـجـ ـح

د ذ ر ز

سـ شـ / ـشـ ـس

صـ ضـ / ـضـ ـص

ط ظ / ـطـ ـط

أ ا

بـ تـ ثـ / ـبـت

جـ حـ خـ / ـجـ ـح

د ذ ر ز

سـ شـ / ـشـ ـس

صـ ضـ / ـضـ ـص

ط ظ / ـطـ ـط

أ ا

بـ تـ ثـ / ـبـت

جـ حـ خـ / ـجـ ـح

د ذ ر ز

سـ شـ / ـشـ ـس

صـ ضـ / ـضـ ـص

ط ظ / ـطـ ـط

أ ا

بـ تـ ثـ / ـبـت

جـ حـ خـ / ـجـ ـح

د ذ ر ز

سـ شـ / ـشـ ـس

صـ ضـ / ـضـ ـص

ط ظ / ـطـ ـط

ACTIVITY 7: Trace the Alphabet in joining positions

أ ا	أ ا
بـ تـ ثـ / ـبـت	بـ تـ ثـ / ـبـت
جـ حـ خـ / ـجـ ح	جـ حـ خـ / ـجـ ح
د ذ ر ز	د ذ ر ز
سـ شـ / ـشـ ـس	سـ شـ / ـشـ ـس
صـ ضـ / ـضـ ـص	صـ ضـ / ـضـ ـص
ط ظ / ـطـ ـط	ط ظ / ـطـ ـط
عـ غـ ـعـ ـغـ غ ـع	عـ غـ ـعـ ـغـ غ ـع
فـ ـفـ ف قـ ـقـ ـق	فـ ـفـ ف قـ ـقـ ـق

ACTIVITY 8: Practice Connecting the following letters. We will add this the group of letters

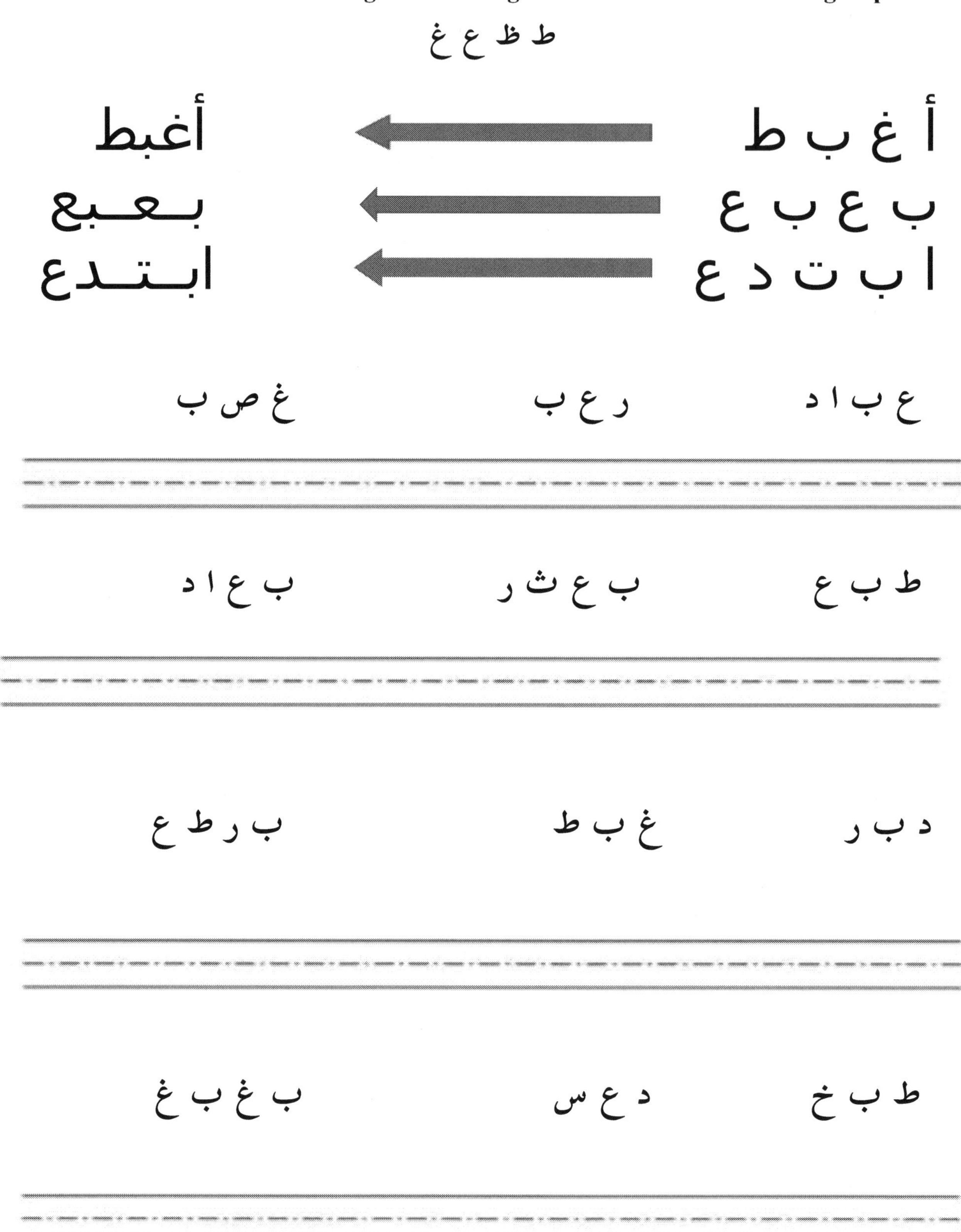

ACTIVITY 9: Trace the Alphabet in joining positions

أ ا

بـ تـ ثـ / ـبـ ـت

جـ حـ خـ / ـجـ ـح

د ذ ر ز

سـ شـ / ـشـ ـس

صـ ضـ / ـضـ ـص

ط ظ / ـطـ ـط

عـ غـ ـعـ ـغـ ـغ ـع

فـ ـفـ ـف قـ ـقـ ـق

كـ ـكـ ـك

لـ ـلـ ـل

مـ ـمـ ـم

نـ ـنـ ـن

أ ا

بـ تـ ثـ / ـبـ ـت

جـ حـ خـ / ـجـ ـح

د ذ ر ز

سـ شـ / ـشـ ـس

صـ ضـ / ـضـ ـص

ط ظ / ـطـ ـط

عـ غـ ـعـ ـغـ ـغ ـع

فـ ـفـ ـف قـ ـقـ ـق

كـ ـكـ ـك

لـ ـلـ ـل

مـ ـمـ ـم

نـ ـنـ ـن

ACTIVITY 10: Practice Connecting the following letters. We will add this the group of letters

ف ق ك ل

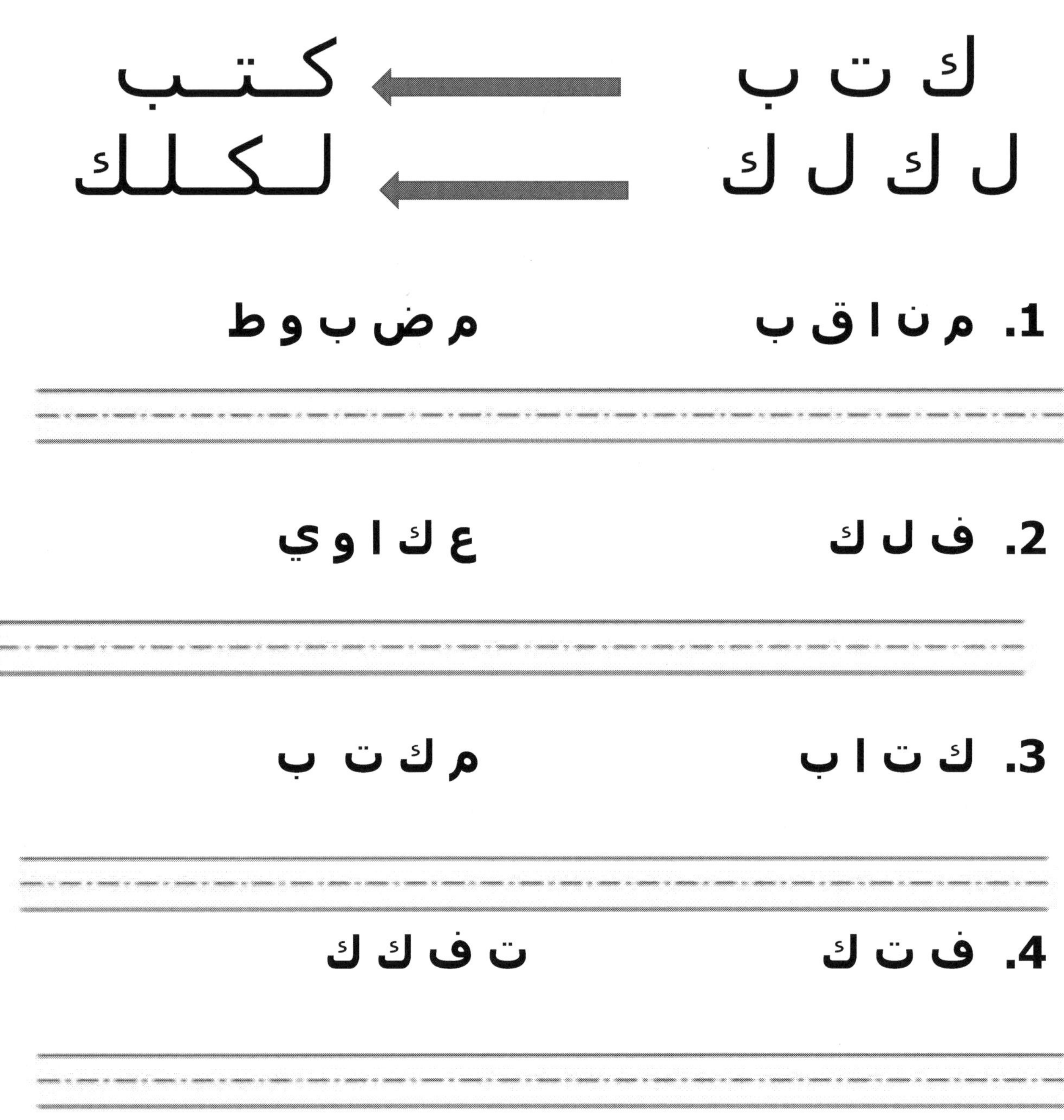

ACTIVITY 11: Trace the Alphabet in joining positions

أ ـا

بـ تـ ثـ / ـبـ ـت

جـ ـحـ ـخـ / ـجـ ـح

د ذ ر ز

سـ شـ / ـشـ ـس

صـ ضـ / ـضـ ـص

ط ظ / ـطـ ـط

عـ غـ ـعـ ـغـ غ ع

فـ ـفـ ـف قـ ـقـ ـق

ك ـكـ ـك

لـ ـلـ ـل

مـ ـمـ ـم

نـ ـنـ ـن

أ ـا

بـ تـ ثـ / ـبـ ـت

جـ ـحـ ـخـ / ـجـ ـح

د ذ ر ز

سـ شـ / ـشـ ـس

صـ ضـ / ـضـ ـص

ط ظ / ـطـ ـط

عـ غـ ـعـ ـغـ غ ع

فـ ـفـ ـف قـ ـقـ ـق

ك ـكـ ـك

لـ ـلـ ـل

مـ ـمـ ـم

نـ ـنـ ـن

ACTIVITY 12: Trace the Alphabet in joining positions

أ ـا

بـ تـ ثـ / ـبـ ـت

جـ حـ خـ / ـجـ ـح

د ذ ر ز

سـ شـ / ـشـ ـس

صـ ضـ / ـضـ ـص

ط ظ / ـطـ ـط

عـ غـ ـعـ ـغـ ـغ ـع

فـ ـفـ ـف قـ ـقـ ـق

كـ ـكـ ـك

لـ ـلـ ـل

مـ ـمـ ـم

نـ ـنـ ـن

هـ ـهـ ـه ه

و ـو

يـ ـيـ ـي

أ ـا

بـ تـ ثـ / ـبـ ـت

جـ حـ خـ / ـجـ ـح

د ذ ر ز

سـ شـ / ـشـ ـس

صـ ضـ / ـضـ ـص

ط ظ / ـطـ ـط

عـ غـ ـعـ ـغـ ـغ ـع

فـ ـفـ ـف قـ ـقـ ـق

كـ ـكـ ـك

لـ ـلـ ـل

مـ ـمـ ـم

نـ ـنـ ـن

هـ ـهـ ـه ه

و ـو

يـ ـيـ ـي

ACTIVITY 13: Practice Connecting the following letters. We will add this the group of letters

م ن هـ و ي

ب ي ا ن ---------------- بـيـان

ي م ش ي ---------------- يـمـشـي

ن م ل ------------------ نـمـل

هـ و ا م ش --------------- هـوامـش

ن ز ي هـ ----------------- نزيـه

س ر هـ ----------------- سره*

م ل م ------------ ملم

م د ي ر ------------ مدير

ل ب ن ا ن -------------- لبنان

م هـ م ا ت ----------------- مهمات

*Note: the هـ is written as a circle when precede by an unsocial letter

ACTIVITY 14: Join these groups of letters to form words

1. هـ و ا ي ا ت ض ا ع

2. ي ج ر ي هـ ب ا ت

3. ف ا ك هـ ن م ي س

4. ي ض ي ع و ز ي ر

ACTIVITY 15: Join these groups of letters to form words

1. م غ ن ي　　　ع ص ف و ر

2. ف ي ل　　　ث ع ل ب

3. ط ب ق　　　ب ر ت ق ا ل

4. ا ل ج و ف　　　د ق ي ق

5. ا ل ج م ل　　　ا ل ح ص ا ن

6. ا ل س ب ا ن خ   ي و س ف ي

7. ب ر ق و ق   ب ق د و ن س

8. خ ص   خ ي ا ر

9. د و ر ي   ش ر ط ي

ACTIVITY 16: Join these groups of letters to form words

1. م ن ط ا د — م ل ز م ا ت

2. ر ب ي ا ن — ط و ي ل

3. ب ح ا ر — س ف ن

4. أ س ت ا ذ — أ ح د

5. م ب ا ن ي — ج م ع ي ا ت

ACTIVITY 17: Join these groups of letters to form words

1) ع ص ف و ر   ي م ا م

2) أ ف ي ا ل   ث ع ل ب

3) أ ط ب ا ق   د ق ي ق

4) ر م ا ن   ب ر ق و ق

5) م و س ي ق ا ر   ف ي ل س و ف

ACTIVITY 18: Join these groups of letters to form words

1. ي ا س م ي ن   ف ل

2. أ ر ز   ب ر ت ق ا ل

3. ي و س ف ي   و ر د ا ت

4. س ق ي ا ن   م س ل س ل

5. د ي د ا ن   ط ا و ل ا ت

Special Case

When ل is followed by the letter ا, (ا + ل) it takes 2 distinctive shapes:

1. The letter ا will be twisted and connected to the base of the ـل if preceded by an unsocial letter, as such:

2. The ا will be place over the tail of the ل, where the Lam is preceded by a social letter or not,

as such: لا

This shape will be the default shape for both cases, in writing, however you need to distinguish the other shape in printed text. لا

Examples:

الإتحـاد	ا لإتـحـا د
دلال	دلال
د لالات	دلالات

ACTIVITY 19: Join these groups of letters to form words

1) ا ل إ ت ح ا د ا ل إ س ت ع د ا د ا ت

2) ا ل إ مـ ت ح ا ن ا ت ا ل ا ض ط ر ا ب ا ت

3) ا ل أ ي ا مـ ا ل ا س ت ع مـ ا ر

4) ا ل إ ب ت ه ا ل ا ت ا ل إ س ت هـ ل ا ل ا ت

1) مـ ح ي ط ا ت ا ل ب ر ت غ ا

ACTIVITY 20: Join these groups of letters to form words

1) ا ل إ س ت ب ي ا ن ا ت — ا ل إ س ت ب ش ا ر ا ت

2) ا ل إ س ت ط ل ا ع — ا ل إ ب ت س ا مـ ا ت

3) ا ل أ ي ت ا مـ — ا ل أ ر ز ا ق

4) ا ل إ س ت ك ا ن ا ت — ا ل إ ع ت ب ا ر ا ت

5) ا ل أ مـ ر ا ض — ا ل أ ك ت ا ف

ACTIVITY 21: Join these groups of letters to form words

1) مـ ن ت د ي ا ت   ا س ت ق ل ا ل   مـ ل ا ب س

2) ت ا س ت غ ف ا ر   مـ ت م ر س   مـ ي ا د ي ن

3) ا ح ت ف ا ل ا ت   مـ ص ا ر ع ا ت   ا ح ت ل ا ل ا ت

4) ط ا و ل ا ت   ا ز د ح ا مـ   ف ي د ي و هـ ا ت

6. ر ب ا ع ي ا ت   ت ل ف ز ي و ن ا ت

ACTIVITY 22: Join these groups of letters to form words

1. مـ ص ر — ك ي مـ ي ت — ج ي ب ت ا ن ا

2. ا ل ع ر ا ق — س و ر ي ا — ل ب ن ا ن

3. إ ي ر ا ن — إ ث ي و ب ي ا — ع مـ ا ن

4. ا ل ي مـ ن — ا ل ك و ي ت — ا ل س ع و د ي

5. ق ط ر — ا ل إ مـ ا ر ا ت — ا ل س و د ا ن

ACTIVITY 23: Join these groups of letters to form words

1) ا ل مـ ن ف ل و ط ي   ت و ف ي ق   ا ل ح ك ي م

2) ن ج ي ب   مـ ح ف و ظ   إ د ر ي س

3) أ ن ي س   مـ ن ص و ر   ي و س ف

4) ن ا هـ د   ص ل ي ح   ن ب ي ل   ر ا غ ب

5) م ي ر ا ل   ا ل ط ح ا و ي   ا ب ر ا هـ ي م

ACTIVITY 24: Join these groups of letters to form words

1. ا ل أ هـ ر ا مـ ا ت   أ ب و   ا ل هـ و ل

2. ا ل أ ق ص ر   ا ل إ س ك ن ر ي

3. س ي ن ا و ي   ا ل د ق هـ ل ا و ي

4. ا ل م ن ص و ر ي   ا ل ف ي و مـ

5. ا ل ق ي ر و ا ن   ط ر ا ب ل س

*__Note__: The shapes ـــة / ة **is** called "Taa Marbouta ".

Phonologically, it represents the sound ت. It occurs only as the final letter in a word, which is identical to the letter ـه, at the end of a word except for the two dots.

Grammatically, it indicates feminine gender in the noun or adjective.

Letters that look similar when connected	
ج ح خ جـ حـ خـ	بـ تـ ثـ نـ يـ ـبـ ـتـ ـثـ ـنـ ـيـ
ر ز	د ذ

ACTIVITY 25: Join these groups of letters to form words

1) ب س ت ا ن　　زهـ ر ة　　ب س ن ت

2) مـ ا ر ي ة　　ك ا مـ ل ة　　ش ي ر و ي ت

3) ن ز ه ة　　و ر ق ة　　ش ج ر ة

4) ر مـ ا ن　　مـ ش مـ ش ة　　ب ط ي خ

5) ن ب ت ة　　م س ر و ر ة　　أ و ر ا ق

Letters that look similar when connected	
ص ض صـ ضـ	س ش سـ شـ
ع غ عـ غـ	ط ظ
ا ل ـا ـلـ	ف ق فـ قـ
	ة ه ـة ـه

LESSON 3

Short Vowels

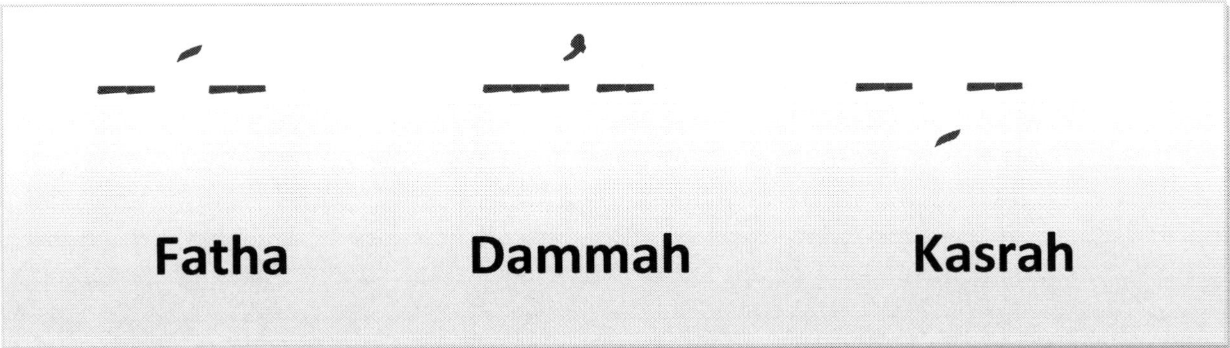

1. In Arabic language alphabet letters come associated with diacritic.
2. marks that represent the short vowels
3. The diacritics are small marks that appear over or under a letter in order to guide you to read it properly.

In this

1. Dammah: is a mini WAW و written above the consonant.

It represents a short vowel as in “Put “.

2. FaTha: is a diagonal mark written above the consonant.

It represents a short vowel as in “Nut “ .

3. Kasra: is a diagonal mark written below the consonant.

It represents a short vowel as in "Pit".

practice reading your Alphabet associated with the short vowels, with your teacher.

أَ	أُ	إِ	بَ	بُ	بِ
تَ	تُ	تِ	ثَ	ثُ	ثِ
جَ	جُ	جِ	حَ	حُ	حِ
خَ	خُ	خِ	دَ	دُ	دِ
ذَ	ذُ	ذِ	رَ	رُ	رِ
زَ	زُ	زِ	سَ	سُ	سِ
شَ	شُ	شِ	صَ	صُ	صِ
ضَ	ضُ	ضِ	طَ	طُ	طِ
ظَ		ظُ		ظِ	

Continue Reading

غِ	غُ	غَ	عِ	عُ	عَ
قِ	قُ	قَ	فِ	فُ	فَ
لِ	لُ	لَ	كِ	كُ	كَ
نِ	نُ	نَ	مـِ	مـُ	مـَ
وِ	وُ	وَ	هـِ	هـُ	هـَ
يِ		يُ		يَ	

Practice with your teacher pronouncing the Arabic alphabet associated with the 3 main short vowels (FaTha, kasrah, Dammahh) through the following table:

Practice reading the following words with your teacher:

Vocabulary			
1. The leap	وَثَــبَ	2. To request	طَلَبَ
3. To hear	سَــمِــعَ	4. To Descend	نَــزَلَ
5. To Do	فَــعَــلَ	6. To Drink	شَرِبَ
7. To Be Full	شَــبِــعَ	8. To Eat	أَكَــلَ
9. To Jump	قَــفَــزَ	10. To Succeed	نَــجَــحَ
11. To Hit	ضَرَبَ	12. To Plant	زَرَعَ
13. To Swallow	بَــلَــعَ	14. To ride	رَكِــبَ

ACTIVITY 1: Listen twice to a list of 10 words that contain short vowels, then decide which short vowel is used in each word and place a mark in the appropriate column. Remember that the three short vowels are ـَ ـُ ـِ which equate to but, put, and hit

ـــِـــ Kasrah	ـــُـــ Dammahh	ـــَـــ FaTha		ـــِـــ Kasrah	ـــُـــ Dammahh	ـــَـــ FaTha	
			6.				1.
			7.				2.
			8.				3.
			9.				4.
			10.				5.

ACTIVITY 2: Listen to a list of 10 Arabic words that contain short vowels. Listen again, and then decide which short vowel is used at the beginning of each word and place a mark in the appropriate column. Each word will be pronounced twice.

ـــِـــ Kasrah	ـــُـــ Dammahh	ـــَـــ FaTha		ـــِـــ Kasrah	ـــُـــ Dammahh	ـــَـــ FaTha	
			.6				(1
			.7				(2
			.8				(3
			.9				(4
			.10				(5

ACTIVITY 3: Listen to a list of 10 Arabic words that contain short vowels. Listen again, and then decide which short vowel is used at the beginning of each word and place a check mark in the appropriate column. Each word will be pronounced twice.

---- Kasrah	---- Dammahh	---- FaTha		--◌-- Kasrah	--◌-- Dammahh	--◌-- FaTha	
			.6				(1
			.7				(2
			.8				(3
			.9				(4
			.10				(5

ACTIVITY 4: Listen to a list of 10 Arabic words that contain short vowels. Listen again, and then decide which short vowel is used at the beginning of each word and place a check mark in the appropriate column. Each word will be pronounced twice.

---- Kasrah	---- Dammahh	---- FaTha		---- Kasrah	---- Dammahh	---- FaTha	
			(6				(1
			(7				(2
			(8				(3
			(9				(4
			(10				(5

ACTIVITY 5: Join the letters based on the rules you learned to form words.

1. ال ا مـ ت ح ا ن   أ غ س ط س   ال ر أ س

2. ال إ ن س ا ن   ال ز مـ ر د   ال ح د ي د

3. ال ب ن ا ت   ال ب س ت ا ن   أ ك ت و ب ر

4. ب ح ي ر ا ت   هـ ا مـ ب ر ج ر   ط ب ي ب

5. مـ س ت ش ف ى   ع ص ف و ر   مـ هـ ن د س

6. ب س ت ا ن   ك ت ا ب   ج ز ر

ACTIVITY 6: Join the letters based on the rules you learned to form words.

1. ا ل إ س ت مـ ا ع ا ت　　　س ي ن م ا

---

2. مـ ر ا د　　　ز م ا ن

---

3. ب ي ا ن ا ت　　　م ر ا د ف ا ت

---

4. ق ا ر ا ت　　　ق ط ر

Long Vowels

- There are three long vowels in Arabic. The Arabic long vowels equate to the English vowels as in **Dad**, as in **Machine**, and as in **Boot**.
- The three letters ا و ى are used as long vowels that is, sustained in pronunciation as twice as the short vowel or held twice as long as the short vowel.
- Note: If ا ، و ، ي carry any of the diacritic mark: FaTha, Dammah, or Kasra, they are considered consonants.
- The Arabic long vowels equate to the English long vowels
- /a/ as in *car* and /æ/as in *Jack*, /i/ as in *jeep*, and /u/ as in *boot*.

*The imitation of your teacher is necessary. Therefore, look at the following table and practice with your teacher.

أَ	ءا	آ	أُ	أو	إِ	ءِ	إيـ	ئِي

بَ	با	بُ	بو	بِ	بي
تَ	تا	تُ	تو	تِ	تي
ثَ	ثا	ثُ	ثو	ثِ	ثي
جَ	جا	جُ	جو	جِ	جي
حَ	حا	حُ	حو	حِ	حي
خَ	خا	خُ	خو	خِ	خي
دَ	دا	دُ	دو	دِ	دي
ذَ	ذا	ذُ	ذو	ذِ	ذي
رَ	را	رُ	رو	رِ	ري
زَ	زا	زُ	زو	زِ	زي
سَ	سا	سُ	سو	سِ	سي
شَ	شا	شُ	شو	شِ	شي

صي	صِ	صو	صُ	صا	صَ
ضي	ضِ	ضو	ضُ	ضا	ضَ
طي	طِ	طو	طُ	طا	طَ
ظي	ظِ	ظو	ظُ	ظا	ظَ
عي	عِ	عو	عُ	عـا	عَ
غي	غِ	غو	غُ	غـا	غَ
في	فِ	فو	فُ	فـا	فَ
قي	قِ	قو	قُ	قا	قَ
كي	كِ	كو	كُ	كا	كَ
لي	لِ	لو	لُ	لا	لَ
مي	مِ	مو	مُ	ما	مَ
ني	نِ	نو	نُ	نا	نَ
هي	هِ	هو	هُ	ها	هَ
وي	وِ	وو	وُ	وا	وَ
يي	يِ	يو	يُ	يا	يَ

ACTIVITY 7: Listen to a List of 10 words that contain long vowels. Listen again and decide which long vowel is used in each word, then place a check mark in the appropriate column.

ي	و	ا		ي	و	ا	
			(6				(1
			(7				(2
			(8				(3
			(9				(4
			(10				(5

ACTIVITY 8: Listen to a list of 10 words that contain long vowels. Listen again and decide which long vowel is used in each word, then place a check mark in

ي	و	ا		ي	و	ا	
			(6				(1
			(7				(2
			(8				(3
			(9				(4
			(10				(5

ACTIVITY 9: Listen to a list of 10 words, which contain either a long or a short vowel. Indicate which type of vowel is used—either long or short—by checking the appropriate column

Long Vowel	Short Vowel		Long Vowel	Short Vowel	
		(6			.1
		(7			.2
		(8			.3
		(9			.4
		(10			.5

ACTIVITY 10: Listen to a series of words, which contain either a long or a short vowel. Indicate which type of vowel is used—either long or short—by checking the appropriate column

Long Vowel	Short Vowel		Long Vowel	Short Vowel	
		.6			(1
		.7			(2
		.8			(3
		.9			(4
		.10			(5

ACTIVITY 11: Listen to a list of 10 words, which contain either a long or a short vowel. Indicate which type of vowel is used—either long or short—by checking the appropriate column

Long Vowel	Short Vowel		Long Vowel	Short Vowel	
		(6			(1
		(7			(2
		(8			(3
		(9			(4
		(10			(5

ACTIVITY 12: Listen to a series of words, which contain either a long or a short vowel. Indicate which type of vowel is used—either long or short—by checking the appropriate column

Long Vowel	Short Vowel		Long Vowel	Short Vowel	
		.6			.1
		.7			.2
		.8			.3
		.9			.4
		.10			.5

ACTIVITY 13: Join the letters based on the rules you learned to form words.

1. مـ و ن ت ا ن ا — ت ل ي ف و ن

2. مـ و ت ي ل — ع د ن ا ن

3. مـ ي ا مـ ي — م ل ي و ن

4. ك و ي ت — ل ن د ن

5. ق ط و س — مـ ك ا ن

Vocabulary List			
Weeks	أَسَابِيــع	Potatos	بَـطاطِس
Psalms	مَزامِير	Famouns	شَـهِير
Dogs	كِلاب	Elephant	فِيـل
Mahatir (Name)	مَـهـاتِير	Mines	مَنـاجِـم

The Shaddah & SuKuun

SuKuun Shaddah

In addition to the three main diacritic marks (FaTha, Dammah, and kasra), there are two more diacritic marks:

1. **The sukuun** سُكُون ْ is a circle-shaped diacritic placed above a letter, which represents the end of a closed syllable (CvC or CvvC).

   It indicates that the consonant, to which it is attached to, is not followed by a vowel.

   Practice with your teacher reading the following examples:

مَـوْتْ	يَـوْمْ	مَـنْ	دُفْ	تِـبْـنْ
Death	Day	Who	Drum	Hay
بَـرْقْ	شَـهْـرْ	مِـنْ	بِنْـتْ	بَـدْوْ
Lightning	Month	From	Girls	Bedouin
تَـمْـرْ	ثَـوْمْ	ثَـوْبْ	مُـنْـذُ	شَـمْـسْ
Dates	Garlic	Dress	Since	Sun

2. Shadda "شَــدَّة" ّ a diacritic formed like a small "w". Shadda represents doubling (or gemination) of a consonant. Where the same consonant occurs twice in a word, with no vowel between. So instead of using **consonant + sukūn + consonant**, the consonant is written only once, and shadda is written above it.

It is functionally equivalent to writing a consonant twice in English, **with the** repetition of a letter twice, but with two different sounds:

a) The first sound of the letter with **"Sukuun",**

b) The second sound with the **associated diacritic**, both with continuity.

*The following table shows the proper way to write the shaddah associated with short vowels.

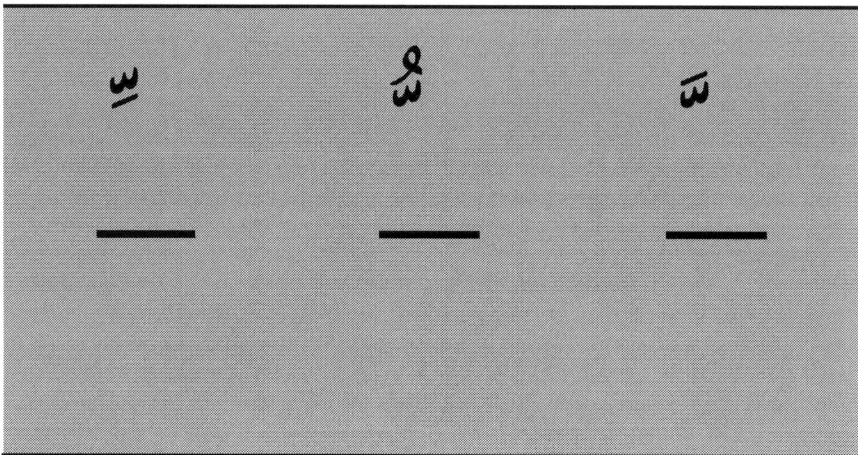

Practice with your teacher reading the following examples:

كَلَّمَ	بَرَّدَ	سلَّـم
كَلْ لَمَ	بَرْ رَد	سلْ لَمَ

صَفَّارة	تُـفَّـاحَة	حَـمَّـل
مُعَلِّم	نقَّـاش	أيـُّوب

ACTIVITY 14: Listen to 14 words read twice. Each word contains one or more of the 6 letters listed below. For each word, circle the letter(s) you recognize, and then check your answers with classmates.

ب	ن	ش	ص	ا	م		ك	ب	ل	ي	ا	ت	
						(8							(1
						(9							(2
						(10							(3
						(11							(4
						(12							(5
						(13							(6
						(14							(7

ACTIVITY 15: You will hear 14 words read twice. Each word contains one or more of the 6 letters listed below. For each word, circle the letter(s) you recognize, and then check your classmates.

ث	ب	ع	غ	ق	ك		ظ	ض	غ	ن	س	ت	
						.8							.1
						.9							.2
						.10							.3
						.11							.4
						.12							.5
						.13							.6
						.14							.7

ACTIVITY 16: Fill in the missing letters in the appropriate form for each letters' position (initial, medial, final, or independent).

....ـــال خ	.6	مـ ...ـطفـى ص	.5	طا....ب ل	.4	سلطا... ن	.3	....طف ق	.2	طب....ب ي	.1
مظ....ر هـ	.12	بير... ت و	.11	م......رسة د	.10	جد.....د ي	.9	قديـ....... م	.8	مديـ...... ر	.7
مت....ف ح	.18	مـ.......هور ش	.17	مـ........تب ك	.16	شـ......رة ج	.15	جامـ ...... ـة ع	14	سبـ... رة و	13

ACTIVITY 17: Listen to your teacher reading a list of 14 Arabic words. Identify and place a checkmark if you hear any of the following letters:

ر	ن	ش	ي	و	ك		ذ	ط	ث	ل	د	ب	
						(8							(1
						(9							(2
						(10							(3
						(11							(4
						(12							(5
						(13							(6
						(14							(7

ACTIVITY 18: You have 24 words. The first letter of each word is not voweled. Your teacher will read each word twice. Listen, and then add the short vowels associated with the first letter only (-- ِ ، -- ُ ، -- َ). Check your answers with your classmate.

6. تـل	5. نـمـل	4. مـن	3. مـمـل	2. مـتـيـن	1. لـم
12. ذراع	11. غضبان	10. مسرور	9. مقبول	8. جيد	7. ممتاز
18. دمشق	17. عصفور	16. يمام	15. طاولة	14. أستاذ	13. معلم
24. ببغاء	23. برتقال	22. برقوق	21. يوسفي	20. خوخ	19. بطيخ

ACTIVITY 19: your teacher will read 28 words, twice each. Listen carefully and then add the short vowels associated with the first letter only (-- ِ ، -- ُ ، -- َ). Check your answers with your classmate.

.7	.6	.5	.4	.3	.2	.1
.14	.13	.12	.11	.10	.9	.8
.21	.20	.19	.18	.17	.16	.15
.28	.27	.26	.25	.24	.23	.22

ACTIVITY 20: Listen to your teacher reading a list of 14 Arabic words. Identify and place a checkmark if you hear any of the following letters:

ذ	ز	ق	ك	م	ن		غ	ث	س	ظ	ذ	ي	
						.8							.1
						.9							.2
						.10							.3
						.11							.4
						.12							.5
						.13							.6
						.14							.7

ACTIVITY 21: Listen to your teacher reading a list of 12 Arabic words. Identify and place a checkmark if you hear any of the following letters:

ض	س	ص	ط	ت	م		ز	د	ع	غ	ذ	ظ	
						(7							(1
						(8							(2
						(9							(3
						(10							(4
						(11							(5
						(12							(6

ACTIVITY 22: Join the letters based on the rules you learned to form words.

1) ث و ب   ا ل ا س ت هـ ل ا ل

2) أ ن ف   ر أ س

3) ش ع ر   ذ ر ا ع

4) ر ك ب   ك ع ب

5) إ ص ب ع   ع ق ل

6) ظ ف ر　　　　أ ذ ن

7) ي د　　　　ع ي ن

8) ك ا ل ي ف و ر ن ي ا　　　　ز ب ي ب

9) ض ب ع　　　　ق ر د

10) ح ا س و ب　　　　م س ج ل

Lesson 3 Vocabulary List

Youth	شَــبَـاب	Big	كَبِــيــر
Door	بَـاب	Tall	طَـوِيـل
People	نَـاس	Cold	بَـارِد
Far	بَـعِـيـد	Elephant	فِـيـل
Handsome	وَجِـيـه	Small	صَغِـيـر
Gorgeous	بَـدِيع	Short	قَصِـيـر
Honest	نَزِيه	Thin	رَقِـيـق

LESSON 4

Hamza هَمْزَة

Hamza ء or glottal stop often does stand as a separate letter in writing. ســاء

It may appear as a diacritic over or under the ا: أ إ لأ لإ

Also, it may appear with و & ي and it looks like that: ئ ؤ, in order to support the Hamzah, depends on the quality of the adjacent vowels (we will cover this point, in details, in lesson 7).

Note: Hamza is pronounced as in "Eaten".

Examples

1. مَلْجَأْ	1) إِبْرَة	1. أُخْت
2. مَاءْ	2) مُؤْلِم	2. أَخ
3. نَبَأْ	3) مــــؤَيـــد	3. أُم
4. مَخْبَأْ	4) أُسْرَة	4. إِخْوَة
5. سَماءْ	5) شاطِئْ	5. رَأَف
6. لَجَأَ	6) شِـــتاء	6. أَنــا
7. سَأَلَ	7) أَمْرِيكا	7. أَنْتَ
8. أُسْـتُرالْيا	8) سَأَمْ	8. إِذاً
9. بَراءَة	9) مَأْرِب	9. أَرْكَنْسا

ACTIVITY 1: Listen to the following 12 words and mark the correct diacritical mark the Hamza is sounded with:

ــِــ	ــُــ	ــَــ		ــِــ	ــُــ	ــَــ	
			(7				.1
			(8				.2
			(9				.3
			(10				.4
			(11				.5
			(12				.6

ACTIVITY 2: Listen to the following 12 words, some of them have Hamza and some do not have. Identify the words that have the Hamza with a mark in the provided space:

Hamza	No Hamza		Hamza	No Hamza	
		.7			.1
		.8			.2
		.9			.3
		.10			.4
		.11			.5
		.12			.6

ACTIVITY 3: Listen to the following 12 words; they all have Hamza in different positions. Indicate the position of the hamza in each word in the table provided:

Beginning	Middle	Final		Beginning	Middle	Final	
			7.				1.
			8.				2.
			9.				3.
			10.				4.
			11.				5.
			12.				6.

ACTIVITY 4: Listen to the following 12 words, some of them have Hamza and some do not have. Identify the words that have the Hamza with a mark in the provided space:

Hamza	No Hamza		Hamza	No Hamza	
		(7			(1
		(8			(2
		(9			(3
		(10			(4
		(11			(5
		(12			(6

ACTIVITY 5: Join the letters to form words in each given sentence.

1) أ ذ ه ب// إ ل ى// ا ل م د ر س ة // ك ل // ي و م//

2) أ ح ب // أ م ي //و // أ ب ي //

3) ع ن د ي// أ خ //و // أ خ ت//

4) أ ح ب// م د ي ن ت ي//

5) ا ل ط ق س // ج م ي ل// ج د ا// ا ل ي و م //

6) أ ب ي // ي ع م ل// م د ي ر// ف ي// ش ر ك ة//

7) أ م ي// ط ب ي ة// ف ي// ا ل م س ت ش ف ى//

8) أ خ ت ي // م ع ل م ة // ف ي// ا ل م د ر س ة // ا ل ث ا ن و ي ة //

The Pausal Form

Arabic words can be pronounced in two ways:

1- Full form, where the word is pronounced in its entirety.

Example: أَنْتَ

Pausal form, where the word is shortened, in particular the word-final short vowel is not pronounced.

Example: أَنْتْ

However, the pausal form is used when there is no interruption or pause after the pronounced, this would include the complete stop at the end of a sentence.

Punctuation Marks in Arabic

Comma	الفاصلة ،
Semicolon	الفاصلة المنقوطة ؛
Question Mark	علامة الاستفهام ؟
Exclamation Mark	! علامة التأثر أو التعجب
Period	النقطة.
Colon	: النقطتان الرأسيتان
Dash	الشرطة-
2 Dashes	- - الشرطتان
Parentheses	) (القوسان
Brackets	] [القوسان الكبيران
Quotation Mark	" " علامتا التنصيص
Suspension Points	...علامة الحذف
Slash, Slant Line	/ خط مائل

ACTIVITY 6: You will hear 20 words. Each word contains either the letter ق or the letter ك. Write the letter you hear in the proper column, then check your answers with those of a classmate.

.5	.4	.3	.2	.1
.10	.9	.8	.7	.6
.15	.14	.13	.12	.11
.20	.19	.18	.17	.16

ACTIVITY 7: You will hear 10 words, each read twice. Each word contains one of these letters:

ه، ك، ق، س، ص، . mark the letters you recognize for each word,. Check your answers with your class partner.

س	ص	ق	ك	هـ	
					.1
					.2
					.3
					.4
					.5
					.6
					.7
					.8
					.9
					.10

The Definite Article أَلْـ

The الـ is a prefix added at the beginning of the Arabic noun to make it definite.

As in English language, the is equivalent to الـــــ

The definite article أَلْـ is always attached to the noun.

The ء of الـ although pronounced but never written.

The لْـ is always pronounced with a sukuun ـــْـــ

1. The Pen	القَلَـمْ	A Pen	قَـلَـمْ
2. The Book	الـكِتَـــابْ	A Book	كِـتَـابْ
3. The House	البَـيْـتْ	A House	بَـيْـتْ
4. The University	الجَـامِـعَـةْ	A University	جَامِـعَـةْ
5. The Farm	الـمَـزْرَعَـةْ	A Farm	مَزْرَعَـةْ
6. The Room	الغُـرْفَـةْ	A Room	غُـرْفَـةْ

Solar and Lunar letters

In Arabic the consonants are divided into two groups, called the sun letters or solar letters (حروف شمسية) and moon letters or lunar letters (حروف قمرية).

> The solar letters assimilate the letter (ل) of a preceding definite article (الـ).

Solar and Lunar words are derived from the fact that the word for 'the sun', pronounced اَلـشَّمْـس ash-shams, assimilates the لـ, while the word for 'the moon', الْـقَـمَـر, does not.

The following table shows the 2 groups of letters:

Solar letters	**Lunar letters**
ت ث / د ذ ر ز س ش ص ض ط ظ / ل ن	أ ب / ح خ / ع غ ف ق ك/ م / ه/ و/ ي

Note: The لـ is assimilated (NOT pronounced) if followed by one of the solar letter:
HOWEVER: THE لـ IS CLEARLY PRONOUNCED IF FOLLOWED BY THOSE LETTERS:

Note: If the original word begins with the letter ج the assimilation of the لـ is *optional*.

Example			
The university	اَلْجَـامِعَـةْ الـجَّـامِعَـةْ	**University**	جَامِعَـةْ

Practice Reading The Following Words With Your Classmates.

19. المَكْتَبْ	13. الأُمْ	7. السَّــيَّــارَةْ	1. الـطَّـالِـبْ
The office	The mother	The car	The student
20. الـبَـيْـتْ	14. الأَبْ	8. النَّـظَّـارَةْ	2. السَّــلَّــةْ
The house	The father	The glasses	The basket
21. الـغُـرْفَـةْ	15. الأُخْـتْ	9. الثَّـلْجْ	3. الرَّخَـاءْ
The room	The sister	**The ice**	Prosperity
22. الكُـرَّاسَـةْ	16. الأَخْ	10. المَنْـزِلْ	4. الثُّـعْـبَانْ
The notebook	The brother	The resident	The serpent
23. الحَدِيـقَـةْ	17. الـمَـزْرَعَـةْ	11. الـبَـابْ	5. الـطَّـبِـيـبْ
The garden	The farm	The door	The physician
الأُذُنْ	الـكُـرْسِـيّْ	المُمَـرِّضْ	التُّـفَّـاحَـةْ
The ear	The chair	The nurse	The apple

The Different Calendars Used In The Middle East - 2018

Horoscopes!	الأشهر الهجرية Hijri 1439	الأشهر السريانية Assyrian 6768	الأشهر القبطية Coptic/ Egyptian 1734 / 6260	الأشهر الميلادية Gregorian calendar
الميزان(Libra)	مُحرَّم	كانون الثاني	طوبة	.1 يَـنـايِـر
العقرب(Scorpio)	صفر	شباط	أمْشير	.2 فِـبْرايِر
القوس(Sagittarius)	ربيع الأول	آذار	برْمهات	.3 مَارِس
الجدي(Capricorn)	ربيع الآخر	نيسان	برمودة	.4 أَبْـرِيل
الدلو(Aquarius)	جُمادى الأول	أيار	بشْنس	.5 مَايُـو
الحو(Pisces)	جمادى الآخر	حزيران	بؤونة	.6 يُـونْـيُـو
الحمل(Aries)	رجب	تموز	أبيب	.7 يُـولْـيُـو
الثور(Taurus)	شعبان	آب	مسرى	.8 أَغُـسْطُسْ
الجوزاء (Gemini)	رمضان	أيلول	توت	.9 سِـبْـتَـمْـبِـر
السرطان(Cancer)	شوّال	تِشْرين الأَول	بابة	.10 أُكْـتُـوبَـر
الأسد(Leo)	ذو القِعدة	تشْرين الثَّاني	هاتور	.11 نُـوفَـمْـبِـر
العذراء (Virgo)	ذو الحِجة	كانون الأول	كِيهك	.12 دِيـسَـمْـبِـر

Chinese year 4716 = 2018

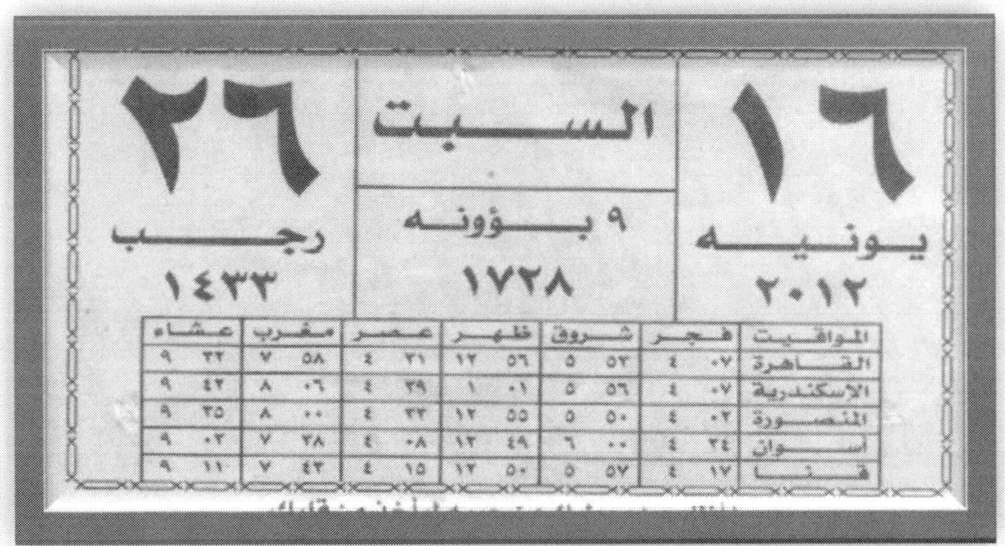

المواقيت	فجر	شروق	ظهر	عصر	مغرب	عشاء
القاهرة	٤ ٠٧	٥ ٥٣	١٢ ٥٦	٤ ٣١	٧ ٥٨	٩ ٣٢
الإسكندرية	٤ ٠٧	٥ ٥٦	١ ٠١	٤ ٣٩	٨ ٠٦	٩ ٤٢
المنصورة	٤ ٠٢	٥ ٥٠	١٢ ٥٥	٤ ٣٣	٨ ٠٠	٩ ٣٥
أسوان	٤ ٣٤	٦ ٠٠	١٢ ٤٩	٤ ٠٨	٧ ٢٨	٩ ٠٢
قنا	٤ ١٧	٥ ٥٧	١٢ ٥٠	٤ ١٥	٧ ٤٣	٩ ١١

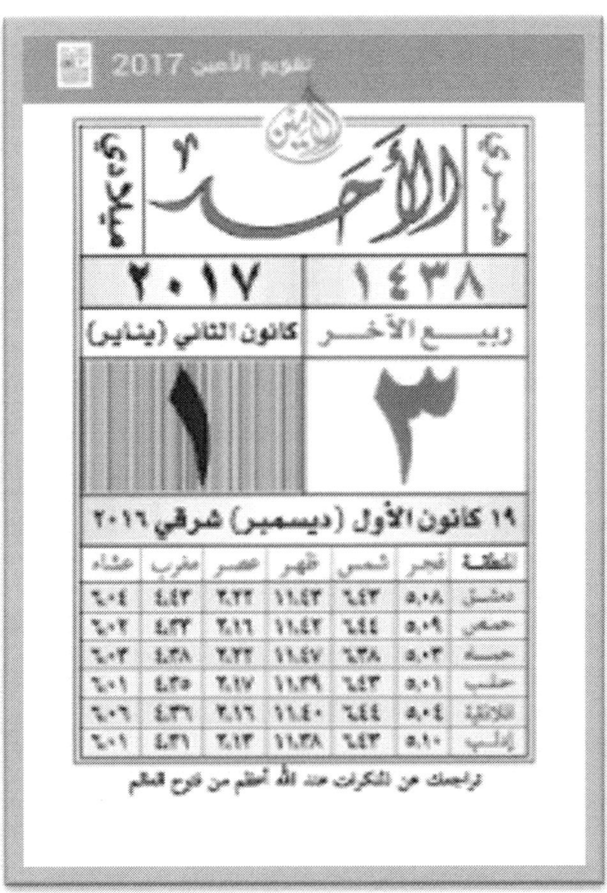

المنطقة	فجر	شمس	ظهر	عصر	مغرب	عشاء
دمشق	٥،٠٨	٦،٤٣	١١،٤٣	٢،٢٢	٤،٤٣	٦،٠٤
حمص	٥،٠٩	٦،٤٤	١١،٤٢	٢،١٦	٤،٣٣	٦،٠٢
حماة	٥،٠٣	٦،٣٨	١١،٤٧	٢،٢٢	٤،٣٨	٦،٠٣
حلب	٥،٠١	٦،٤٣	١١،٣٩	٢،١٧	٤،٣٥	٦،٠١
اللاذقية	٥،٠٤	٦،٤٤	١١،٤٠	٢،١٦	٤،٣٦	٦،٠٦
إدلب	٥،١٠	٦،٤٣	١١،٣٨	٢،١٣	٤،٣١	٦،٠١

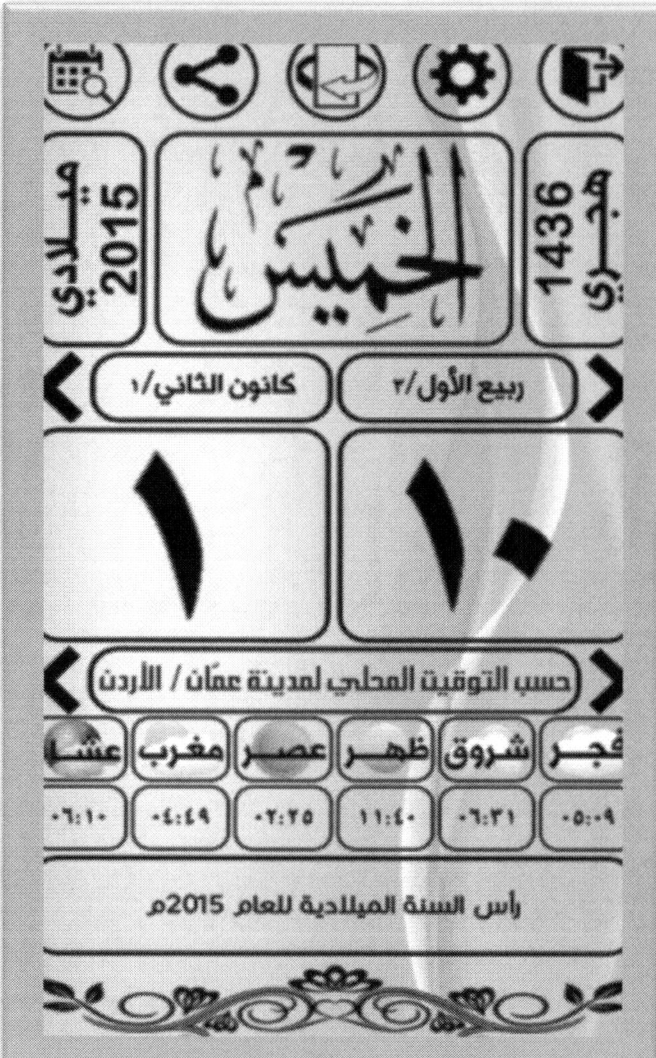
ميلادي 2015
الخميس
1436 هجري
كانون الثاني/١
ربيع الأول/٢
١
١٠
حسب التوقيت المحلي لمدينة عمّان / الأردن
فجر
شروق
ظهر
عصر
مغرب
عشا
٠٥:٠٩
٠٦:٣١
١١:٤٠
٠٢:٢٥
٠٤:٤٩
٠٦:١٠
راس السنة الميلادية للعام 2015م

١٤٣٥ هجري
الأثنين
٢٠١٤
ربيــــع الأول
كانون الثاني (ينـاير)
٢
١
٣
١
٣١ كانون الأول (ديسـمبر) شرقي ٢٠١٣
المنطقة فجر شمس ظهر عصر مغرب عشاء
دمشق ١٠,٥ ٤٢,٦ ٤٧,١١ ٣٠,٢ ٥٣,٤ ١٢,٦
حمص ٧,٥ ٤٤,٦ ٤٦,١١ ٢٤,٢ ٤٣,٤ ١١,٦
حماه ٥,٥ ٣٨,٦ ٥٣,١١ ٣٢,٢ ٤٨,٤ ١٣,٦
حلب ٣,٥ ٤٣,٦ ٤٤,١١ ٢٥,٢ ٤٥,٤ ١٠,٦
اللاذقية ٦,٥ ٤٣,٦ ٤٤,١١ ٢٥,٢ ٤٧,٤ ١٢,٦
دير الزور ٥١,٤ ٣٦,٦ ٢٧,١١ ٩,٢ ٢٨,٤ ٥١,٥
عيد المولد النبوي الشريف (هـ)

Vocative Particle

1. The vocative particles are words used to call someone.
2. In general, there are 7 vocative particles in Arabic, some are used to call the near persons and some for the far persons. We are going to learn only one of the **7**, which is used for the near persons, and it is the most commonly used article.

This vocative particle is (يَـــا)

3. The vocative particle replaces the supposed verb of call, which is eliminated from the sentence structure.
4. The noun following the vocative particle, always takes the sign of the nominative case (Damma in case of singular noun) , without tanwin.

Examples	
I call Ahmad	يـــا أَحْمَدُ
I call Nadia	يـــا نَادِيَةُ
I call the teacher	يـــا أُسْتَاذُ

*Practice calling your classmates and your teacher using the vocative particle!

Note: The sequence اا **is represented by the sign**

(madda) written over an alif like this

Examples	
1. **Relics**	آثــارْ
2. **Quran**	قـــُـرْآنْ
3. **Thousands**	آلافْ
4. **Amen**	آمِينْ
5. **Now**	الآنْ
6. **Mirror**	مِرْآةْ
7. **Minarets**	مَآذِنْ

Lesson 4 Vocabulary List

1. Mother	أُمْ	18. Father	أَبْ
2. Brother	أَخْ	19. Sister	أُخْتْ
3. Physician	طَبيب / ة	20. Nurse	مُمَرِض / ة
4. Ear	أُذُنْ	21. Snake	ثُـعْبـانْ
5. Mouth	فَـمْ	22. Duck	بَـطَّـةْ
6. Hand	يَـدْ	23. Cow	بَـقَـرَةْ
7. Eye	عـيْنْ	24. Lion	أَسَـدْ
8. Hair	شَـعْـرْ	25. Chick	كَـتْكوتْ
9. Watermelon	بَطِّـيـخْ	26. Chicken	دَجـاجَـة / فَـرْخَة
10. Apple	تُـفَّـاحَـةْ	27. Rooster	دِيـكْ
11. Orange	بُرتُـقـالَةْ	28. Teacher	مُعَـلِّـمْ
12. Carrots	جَزَرْ	29. Notebook	كُـرَّاسَـةْ
13. Tomato	طَـمـاطِـم	30. Pen	قَـلَـمْ
14. A House	بَـيْـتْ	31. A Book	كِـتـابْ
15. A Farm	مَزْرَعَـةْ	32. A University	جامِعَـةْ
16. Bag	حَـقِـيـبَـة	33. A Room	غُرْفَةْ
17. The Library	المَكْـتَـبَـة	34. **Garden**	حَدِيـقَـةْ

35. Friend	صاحِب	**49.** Sound	صَوْتْ
36. Farm	مَزْرَعَة	**50.** Pretty / Beautiful	جَميل/ ة
37. Story	قِصَّة	**51.** Clean	نَظيف/ة
38. Butterfly	فَراشَة	**52.** Gold	ذَهَبْ
39. Color	لَوْن	**53.** Sail	شِراع
40. To Draw	رَسَمَ	**54.** Boat	قارِب
41. To Eat	أَكَلَ	**55.** Nurse	مُمَرِّض / ة
42. Needle	إِبْرَة	**56.** Relics	آثـارْ
43. Shelter	مَلْجَأْ	**57.** Quran	قُـرْآنْ
44. Painful	مُؤْلِم	**58.** Thousands	آلافْ
45. Hideout	مَخْبَأْ	**59.** Amen / Amon	آمين
46. Sky	سَماءْ	**60.** Now	الآن
47. Winter	شِتاء	**61.** Mirror	مِرْآة
48. Innocence	بَراءَةْ	**62.** Minarets	مَآذِن

LESSON 5

Gender in Nouns

- In Arabic, nouns are either masculine or feminine.
- The gender of animate nouns is based on their meaning.
- Even the nouns not referring to people, **the inanimate, objects, animals, and abstracts** are subjectively given a gender.

Examples: Learn new vocabulary							
MASCULINE				**FEMININE**			
Animate		**Inanimate/ Objects, animals, Abstracts**		**Animate**		**Inanimate/ Objects, animals, Abstracts**	
Father	1. أبْ	Bird	1. طائِر	Mother	1. أُمّ	Table	1. طَاوِلَة
Mister	2. سَيِّدْ	Moon	2. قَمَرْ	Lady	2. سَيِّدَة	Library	2. مَكْتَبَة
Student	3. طالِبْ	PC	3. حاسُوبْ	Student	3. طالِبَةْ	Fruit	3. فَاكِهَةْ
Boy	4. وَلَدْ	Train	4. قِطارْ	Girl	4. بِنْتْ	Table	4. مِنْضَدَةْ
Teacher	5. مُعَلِّمْ	Lane	5. طابورْ	Teacher	5. مُعَلِّمَة	Carpet	5. سَجَّادَة
Engineer	6. مُهَنْدِس	Future	6. مُسْتَقْبَل	Engineer (F)	6. مُـهَـنْـدِسَـة	Idea	6. فِكْرَة

Taa' Marbouta ة ، ـــــة

- The feminine nouns are mostly formed by adding ة at the corresponding masculine nouns.
- Most of country names are feminine. Very few are masculine.

Except: **المغرب ، الأردُن ، العراق ، السودان ، لُبنان، الكويت،** are masculine country names.

- ة applies to most professions to transform them to feminine.

	Masculine	Feminine
1) Physician	طَبيبْ	طَبيبَة
2) Teacher	مُدَرِّس	مُدَرِّسَة
3) Worker	عامِل	عامِلَة
4) Farmer	فَلّاحْ	فَلّاحَة
5) Journalist	صَحَفِيّ	صَحَفِيَّة
6) Engineer	مُهَنْدِس	مُهَنْدِسَة

However, not all feminine nouns do have a corresponding masculine nouns.

Examples - New Vocabulary	
1) **Newspaper**	جَـريـدَة
2) **Tree**	شَـجَـرَة
3) **Rug**	سَـجّـادَة
4) **Table**	طاوِلَة

ACTIVITY 1: Listen to ten words read by your teacher. Determine whether the words are feminine or masculine. If a word is feminine, indicate which type of feminine: feminine with taa' marbouta or feminine by meaning.

Masculine	Feminine by meaning	Feminine with ة	
			.1
			.2
			.3
			.4
			.5
			.6
			.7
			.8
			.9
			.10

Demonstrative Pronouns For (Nearby) Distance

هٰذَا : means 'This' for masculine singular, It is called the demonstrative pronoun in grammar. It is pronounced هَاذَا but is written without the first /alif/ as such: هٰذَا

Feminine Singular	Masculine Singular	Singular Demonstrative pronouns for nearby
هـٰـذِه	هٰذَا	أسماء إشارة للقريب

Dagger Alif

In a few very common words, the long vowel ا is **NOT** represented with the letter alif after the consonant but with the sign written over the consonant. This sign is a short vertical stroke with the appearance of a small ◌ٰ and is called "dagger alif ".

It is written like that: هٰـذَا

Examples

هٰذَا كِتَابٌ	هٰذَا بَابٌ	هٰذِهِ سَيَّارَة	هٰذِه نَجْمَة
This is a book	This is a door	This is a car	This is a star

ACTIVITY 1: Apply the proper demonstrative pronoun to the following words, then read each word appropriately. Practice with your teacher and classmates.

هذا طبيب	9) طَبيب	هذه طاولة	1) طاوِلَة
	10) فَلّاحـَة		2) جَرِيدَة
	11) صَحَفِيَّة		3) عامِلَة
	12) فلّاح		4) صَحـفِيّ
	13) طَبيبَة		5) مُدَرِّس
	14) مُهَنْدِس		6) مُهَنْدِسَة
	15) شَجَرَة		7) عَامِل
	16) مُدَرِّسَة		8) سَجَّادَة

ACTIVITY 2: Practice with your teacher asking "what is this? "in Arabic is. Create the question and the answer of each item in the box opposite to each picture.

What ـمـــا

سَيَّارة قَلْم شَمْس كُرَّاسَة شَمْسِيَّة رادْيو حاسوب	
Masculine	
	- ما هَذا يا سَمير؟ What is this Samir? - هذا قَمَرْ This a moon
	____________ ____________
	____________ ____________
	____________ ____________

Feminine	
	ما هذه يا سمير؟ --------------
	-------------- --------------
	-------------- --------------
	-------------- --------------

Singular Personal Pronouns

I		أَنـــــــَا	
He	هُــوَ	You M.	أَنـْتَ
She	هِــيَ	You F.	أَنْتِ

I am a student	أَنــا طــــالِــبْ
You are tall	أَنــْتَ طَويلْ
You are beautiful	أَنـْـتِ جَمـيـلَـةْ
He is a student	هـُــوَ طالِـبْ
She is a student	هِـــيَ طالِـبـَةْ

Assimilation

Assimilation means integration.

There is a Hamzah called (هَمْزَةُ الوَصْل) that is pronounced at the beginning of a sentence but is <u>never written</u>, as in the words اِسْم، / اِبْنَة / اِبْن and in some imperatives verbs اُكْتُبْ/ اِرْفَعْ / اِفْتَحْ .
This type of hamza <u>leads to the assimilation</u>. Examples:

هَذا الْبَيْتْ
This hamza is not pronounced (slurred)
اَلْبَيْت كَبِـيرْ
The word بيت is at the beginning of the sentence. It has the definite article الـ.   **the Hamza is pronounced.**

The two words are slurred (glided) together to aid pronunciation and "flow" of the language;

There is a second type of Hamza that is both <u>written and pronounced</u> (هَمْزَةُ القَطْع) in words such as:

You M.	أَنْتَ	I	أَنا
This hamza is pronounced			

أَسْـكُـنُ (في البَـيْـتِ الجَـديـد)	
This hamza is not pronounced	**This hamza is pronounced**

Lesson 5 Vocabulary List

1. Physician	طَبِيبْ / ة	18. Table	طَاوِلَة
2. Teacher	مُدَرِّس / ة	19. Library	مَكْتَبَة
3. Worker	عامِل / ة	20. Fruit	فَاكِهَةْ
4. Farmer	فَلاَّحْ / ة	21. Table	مِنْضَدَة
5. Journalist	صَحَفِيٌّ / ة	22. Carpet	سَجَّادَة
6. Engineer	مُهَنْدِسْ / ة	23. Idea	فِكْرَة
7. Professor	أُسْتَاذْ / ة	24. Girl	بِنْتْ
8. Teacher	مُعَلِّمْ / ة	25. Girl	فـتـاة
9. Student	طالِبَ / ة	26. Sun	شَمْس
10. Mister / Lady	سَيِّدَ / ة	27. Moon	قَمَرْ
11. PC	حاسُوبْ	28. Future	مُسْتَقْبَل
12. Train	قِطارْ	29. Boy	وَلَدْ
13. Lane	طابورْ	30. Student	طالِبْ
14. Bird	طائِر	31. I	أنـــَـــا
15. Umbrella	شَمْسِيَّة	32. You M.	أنــْـتَ
16. Computer	حاسوب	33. You F.	أَنْتِ
17. Radio	رادْيُو	34. I reside	أنا أسْكنُ

LESSON 6

Prepositions حُروف الجَر

Arabic prepositions mostly have a fixed pronunciation regardless of their position in the sentence. They could be attached To Nouns or Pronouns. The table below has the 6 most popularly used prepositions.

Inside In	في	**from // some of // one of**	مِنْ	***About// Away from* something or someone.**	عَنْ
Like //as	الكافُ (كـ)	***by/ with/ in* or *at***	الباء (بـ)	***Reason // possession.***	اللام (لـ)

Examples – Learn new Vocabulary	
The physician is at the clinic.	.1 الطَّبيب في العِيادَة
A big table is in the room	.2 في الغُـرْفَة، طاوِلَة كَبِـيرَة
The article is in the newspaper.	.3 المَقالْ في الجَرِيدَة

The Nunation or Tanwin (final post-nasalized)

The Nunation happened with the three main diacritics.

They are doubled at the end of a word to indicate that the vowel is followed by the consonant **n**.

These are known as tanwīn (تنوين). *Tanwin* gives a distinct pronunciation to the word.

They are pronounced as follows:		
With FaTha: **An**	With Kasrah: **In**	With Dammahh: **On**
ـًــــ	ـٍــــ	ـٌــــ

- Tanwin has (grammar and meaning) references.
- *Tanwin* is the indefinite marker of nouns and adjectives in Arabic. As in English, 'a' and 'an'.
- Tanwin varies according to the word position in the sentence.
- The *tanwin* is replaced by the corresponding default diacritical mark.

The definite article ال and Nunation are **NOT** to be combined.
Nunation is to indicate the absence of the definite article الـ

Note: When Tanwin is added to a word that has the ending case " *FaTha* ", *An* " *Alif* " (ا) *is re*quired to be added after the *tanwin.*

Examples	
مُدَرِّسٌ	المُدَرِّسُ
مُدَرِّسٍ	المُدَرِّسِ
مُدَرِّساً	المَدَرِّسَ

Exception: *If the word* *ends* *with a ta-marbuTah* (ـة / ة /)

or

with *hamzah* (ء) that is preceded by *alif* (ا),

an " Alif " (ا) is ***NOT*** required to be added after the *tanwin.*

Examples

Evening	مَساءً	1. مَســَاءْ
Basket	سَلةً	2. سَـلـَّـة
Air	هـَـواءً	3. هَوَاءْ
Water	مَــاءً	4. مَاءْ
Part	جُـزْءًا	5. جُزْءْ
Warmth	دِفْءاً	6. دِفْءْ

Note:

- *Tanwin* is sometimes used strictly for meaning emphasis.
- *Tanwin* is employed only in the formal use of the language.
- Native speakers of the language are expected to use it in a formal setting.

However, *tanwin* is still used colloquially, *with* greeting words and other frequently used words, such as:

Hello	مَرْحَــبًا	Hello	أَهْلاً
Welcome	أَهْلاً وَسَهْلاً	Thanks	شُكْراً
Also	أَيْضاً	**verb** think nothing of it **interjection** You are welcome! Pardon me!	عَفْواً
Normally	عَادَةً	Approximately	تَقْرِيباً
Really, truly, Actually	فِعْلاً	Together	مَعَاً
Damn	تَباً	Instead	بَدَلاً
Never	أَبَداً	Immediately	حَالاً

Note:

As for right now, do not worry about when to use *Tanwin*.
You are only expected to recognize these "grammatical endings" when you hear them.

Activity 1: Listen to 10 Arabic words with different *nunation* ending. Mark the ending associated with each word in the table provided.

An	In	On	
ـَــ	ـِــ	ـُــ	
			1)
			2)
			3)
			4)
			5)
			6)
			7)
			8)
			9)
			10)

Activity 2: Listen to 10 sentences with words that have different *nunation* ending. Mark the ending *tanwin* associated with each word you recognize in the table provided.

An	In	On	
ـًــ	ـٍــ	ـٌــ	
			(1
			(2
			(3
			(4
			(5
			(6
			(7
			(8
			(9
			(10

Activity 3: You will hear 15 words read by your teacher, each word is missing one of these letters: ض, ف, ق, د , ك , represented by a blank. Determine what letter is missing, and write it in its correct form (initial, medial, final, or independent). Each word will be read twice.

5) ـــــــ قيقة	4) ـــــ اميرا	3) فلا ـــــــ ل	2) ـــــــ فدع	1) بيـ ـــــ
10) فيلاديل ــ ـيا	9) تـ ــ ساس	8) مـ ـــ ريد	7) مـ ـــــ تاح	6) دقيـ ــ
15) مـ ـــ ـــ ان	14) ـــ ـلو	13) ـــــــ فتة	12) مـ ـــــ نن	11) فل ــ ل

Activity 6: Listen to 15 words with different *nunation* ending. Mark the ending associated with each word in the table provided.

An	In	On	
ــــً	ــــٍ	ــــٌ	
			1)
			2)
			3)
			4)
			5)
			6)
			7)
			8)
			9)
			10)
			11)
			12)
			13)
			14)
			15)

Activity 4: Listen to 10 words with different *nunation* ending. Mark the ending associated with each word in the table provided.

An	In	On	
ـــــً	ـــــٍ	ـــــٌ	
			1.
			2.
			3.
			4.
			5.
			6.
			7.
			8.
			9.
			10.

ACTIVITY 5: Listen to 10 words with different *nunation* ending. Mark the ending associated with each word in the table provided.

An	In	On	
ـــــً	ـــــٍ	ـــــٌ	
			1.
			2.
			3.
			4.
			5.
			6.
			7.
			8.
			9.
			10.

Activity 5: Add the definite article ال to each word in the table and decide how to read the word (apply what you have learned about Solar and lunar letters).
Then add the 3 types of Nunation to each word and decide the needed changes. (What should you do to the definite article before adding Tanwin?)

----ٍ	----ٌ	----ً	الـ	
				1. كَبـيـرْ
				2. ذَيْلْ
				3. طاوِلَةْ
				4. لُغَةْ
				5. أبْ
				6. خَيْرْ
				7. والِدَةْ
				8. صَديقْ
				9. زَمِيلْ
				10. دَلْوْ
				11. أخ
				12. قَلَمْ
				13. مُـعَلِّـمْ
				14. سَجّـادَةْ

Activity 7: You will hear 20 words with different nunation ending. Decide the type of nunation ending then place a checkmark in the proper column.

ـــــٍ	ـــــٌ	ـــــً	
			.1
			.2
			.3
			.4
			.5
			.6
			.7
			.8
			.9
			.10
			.11
			.12
			.13
			.14
			.15
			.16
			.17
			.18
			.19
			.20

Activity 8: Join the letters to for words in the given sentences.

Join the following letters to form words and sentences.
1) أ ن ا // م ن // ن ب ر ا سك ا//
2) أ ن ت // أ خ ي //
3) أ م ر ي ك ا // ك ب ي ر ة //
4) أ ب ي// ق و ي//
5) أ م ي // ت ع م ل//
6) ا ل ب ي ت // ك ب ي ر//
7) ا س م ي // ن د ي م //
8) أ ح ب // ج د ي // و // ج د ت ي //
9) ا ل مـَ د ر س ة // ك ب ي ر ة //
10) ز و ج ت ي // ج م ي ل ة // ج د ا //
11) أ ن ا // م ن / أ م ر ي ك ا //
12) ا ل ع ا ل م // أ ص ب ح // ص غ ي ر //

Greetings

Dialogue 1: Greeting

مِدْحَـتْ	صَباحُ اَلْـخَيْـر يـا سَعِـيد
سَعِـيـدْ	صَباحُ النُّور يا مِدْحَتْ
مِـدْحَـت	كَـيْـفَ الحَالْ اليَـوْمْ ؟
سعيد	أَنـا بِـخَـيْـر، و أَنْـتَ؟
مِدحت	أنا أيْـضاً بِخَـيْـر و الحمدُ لِلّه

Medhat: Good morning Saiid, Saiid: Good morning Medhat, Medhat: How are you today? , Saiid: I'm fine and you, Medhat: I am fine, praise be to God

Communication Skills: practice with your teachers and classmates

Dialogue 2: Greeting

بُـثَـيْـنَـة	مَرْحباً يا حَـنانْ، كَيفَ الحالْ اليَوْمْ؟
حَنَـــان	مَرْحَباً يا بُـثَـيْـنَـة، أنا بِخَـيْر و الحَمْدُ لِلَّه. وأَنْـتِ؟
بُـثَـيْـنَـة	أنا أيـْضاً بِخَيْـر وَ الـحَـمْـدُ لِلَّهِ.

Bothainah: Hello Hanan, how are you today? Hanan: Hello Bothainah: I am fine praise be to God "Al-Hamdu Lillaah", And you, Bothainah: I am fine too, praise be to God "Al-Hamdu Lillaah".

Communication Skills: practice with your teachers and classmates

Dialogue 1 & 2 Vocabulary

1. Morning	صَباحُ	2. Status	الحَالْ
3. Good	خَيْـرْ	4. Today	اليَوْمْ
5. And	وَ	6. Light	النُّور
7. You (f)	أنتِ	8. Praise be to God	الحَمْدُ لِلَّهِ

Activity 9 a : Re-write Dialogue 1:

Activity 9 b : Re- Write dialogue 2

Activity 10: Answer the following questions in Arabic:

1. **How do you say Hello in Arabic?**

2. **How can you say how are you in Arabic?**

3. **How would you reply to the question: How are you, in Arabic?**

4. **How to say" I am fine as well" , in Arabic?**

The Nisba Adjective / The relative يّ

Adjectives derived from nouns: When we add the relative يّ (With Shaddah) to a country name, it will create the word for nationality which will be an adjective to the noun that precedes it.

* If we create the nationality for feminine , a ة must be added **after** the يّ.

In addition, the relative يّ is used to create a **"relative adjective"**, so when we want to derive an adjective from a noun we also use the relative يّ.

The rule: If a word is ending with ا ، يا ، ة ; , these endings must be dropped then the relative يّ is added.

If the ountry name begins with the definite article الـ; the الـ **must** be dropped as well.

Examples for Case A

Nationality	Feminine Adjective	Masculine Adjective	The Country name	
Egyptian	مِصْرِيَّة	مِصْرِيّ	مِصْر	Egypt
American	أَمْرِيكِيَّة	أَمْرِيكِيّ	أَمْرِيكَا	America
Lebanese	لُبْنَانِيَّة	لُبْنَانِيّ	لُبْنَانْ	Lebanon
Japanese	يابانيَّة	يابانيّ	يابانْ	Japan
Korean	كُورِيَّة	كُورِيّ	كُورِيَا	Korea
German	ألمانيَّة	ألْمانيّ	ألمانيا	Germany
Chinese	صينيَّة	صينيّ	الصِّين	China
Malian	مـالـيَّة	مـالِـيّ	مـالي	Mali

Examples for **Case B**

Meaning	Feminine Adjective	Masculine Adjective	The word	
Scholastic	مَدْرَسِيَّة	مَدْرَسِيّ	مَدْرَسَة	*School*
Cubic /al	مُكَعَّبِيَّة	مُكَعَّبِيّ	مُكَعَّب	*Cube*
Religious	دِينِيَّة	دِينِيّ	دِين	*Religion*
African	إفْريقيَّة	إفْريقيّ	إفْريقْيا	*Afraica*

ACTIVITY 12: Read the sentences below and create the nationalities in the opposite column. Check your answers with your classmate. The first one is done for you.

چــيمس أمْريكـــــيّ	چــيمس مِنْ أمْريكا (1
	باسِـل مِنْ سُورِيا (2
	مَجدي مِنْ مِصْر (3
	نادية مِنْ المَغْرِبْ (4
	مُصْطفى مِنْ الأُرْدُنْ (5
	إلِيزابيث مِنْ بريطانيا (6
	صوفيَّا مِنْ كَنَدا (7
	أمجد مِنْ الكُوَيْتْ (8
	چيمس مِنْ نيوزيلانْدا (9
	زيــْـنب مِنْ إثــْيــوبْـيا (10
	مَنار مِنْ سُوريَّا (11
	جاسِم مِنْ العِراق (12

Dialogue 3: Introduction

رانْـيـا: صَباحُ الخَيْـرْ يا سَـمِيرْ

سَمـيـر: صَباحُ الخَيْر يـا رَانْـيـا

رانْـيـا: مَـنْ هَذِهِ يا سَمِـيـر؟

سَمـيـر: هِيَ الأُسْتـاذَةُ مَاجِدَة، وَ هِيَ مِصْرِيَّـةٌ.

رانْـيـا: وَ مَنْ هَذا يا سميـر؟

سَمـيـر: هُـوَ الأُسْتاذ صابِر وَ هُوَ مِصْرِيٌّ أَيْضاً.

Good morning Samir, Good morning Rania, who is this Samir?, This is professor Magedah, and she is Egyptians, and who is this?, This is professor Saber and he is Egyptian too.

Communication Skills: Practice with your partner, switch roles 4 times, then take turns and practice with another pair.

Activity 11 : Re- Write Dialogue 3:

Activity 12: Translate the following sentences:

1. My room is cubical

2. I have a scholastic book.

3. My friend is from Morocco.

4. This book is religious.

5. This professor is from Britain.

6. My father is Mexican.

7. My mother is Russian

The Pronoun of Separation

This is a car	هذه سَيَّارَةْ	**This is a pen**	هذا قَـلَمْ
This is a notebook	هذه كُـرَّاسَةْ	**This is a dress**	هذا ثَـوْبْ

Now, how to say: This is the pen.

This is the car	هَذِهِ هِيَ السَّـيَّـارَةْ	This is the pen	هَذا هُـوَ الْقَـلَمْ
This is the notebook	هَذِهِ هِـيَ الكُـرَّاسَـةْ	This is the dress	هَـذَا هُـوَ الثَـوْبْ

As you have noticed, the pronoun هو or هي has been inserted between هذا and القلم / الكراسة.

When هذا or هذه are followed by a definite noun form the meaning هذا القلم / هذه الكراسة which means "this pen" / this notebook.

In order to say, "This is the pen" or "This is the notebook", we must insert the equivalent pronoun, in this case is هو / هي , between هذا and القلم.

This inserted pronoun is called the **"pronoun of separation"** (ضميرُ الفصْل).

Note 1: If the phrase is in plural, then the plural pronouns are used accordingly. We will see more examples when we learn the plural.
Note 2: the pronoun of separation is sometimes optional. When the demonstratives are followed by the construction form "idaafa", not a noun with a definite article, the pronoun of separation is optional, though it is still used to give the sense of emphasis. We will talk about the construction form "Idafa" in details in later lessons

Examples	
1) This is the new student's notebook	هَـذِهِ كُرَّاسَةُ الطَّالِبِ الجَـدِيدْ
This is the new student's notebook	هذه هِيَ كُرَّاسَةُ الطَّالِبِ الجَدِيدْ
2) How is the boy's status?	كَـيْـفَ حَـالُ الوَلَـدْ؟
How is the boy's status?	كَـيفَ هُـوَ حَـال الولد؟ هو is optional because it is followed by the construction form Idaffa

Lesson 6 Vocabulary List

1. Morning	صَباحُ	20) Status	الحَالْ
2. As well	أَيْـضاً	21) Today	اليَوْمْ
3. Good	اَلْخَيْـر	22) Light	النُّور
4. And	و	23) Praise be to God	الحَمْدُ لِلَّهِ
5. Article	المقال	24) New	جديد /ة
6. Newspaper	الجريدة	25) Hello	مَرْحَـبًا
7. Hello	أَهْلاً	26) Welcome	أَهْلاً وَسَهْلاً
8. You are welcome!/ Pardon me!	عَفْواً	27) Really, truly, Actually	فِعْلاً
9. Together	مَعَاً	28) Normally	عَادَةً
10. Approximately	تَقْريباً	29) Also	أَيْضاً
11. Thanks	شُكْراً	30) Damn	تَباً
12. Instead	بَدَلاً	31) Never	أَبَداً
13. Immediately	حَالاً	32) Evening	مَساءً
14. The Chair	الكُرْسِيّ	33) Basket	سَلةً
15. Water	مَـاءً	34) Air	هَـواءً
16. Sleep	نَوْمْ	35) Prosperity	الرَّخَـاءْ
17. Tail	ذَيْلْ	36) Glasses	النَّظَّارَةْ
18. Colleague	زَميلْ	37) Language	لُغَةْ
19. Father / Mother	والِدَ / ةْ	38) Good	خَيْرْ

LESSON 7

Read the following sentences with your class partner and your teacher. Take extra notes if necessary.

1) أنا مِنْ وِلايَة تِكْساس

I am from the state of Texas.

2) أُسْـرَتي مِنْ ولاية كَاليفورنيا

My family is from California.

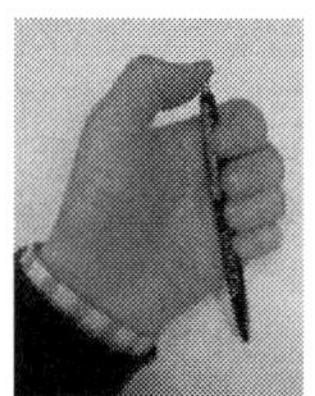

3) مَعِـــي قَلَـم

With me (I have) a pen

4) عِنْدي سَــيَّــارَة

At me (I have) a car

5) أَنا طَــالِبٌ

I am a student

(1 هذا مَكْتَبِـــي

This is my desk

أنا طَالِبَة فِـــي الجَامِعَة

I am a (f) Student at the university

أنا أَلْعَــبُ كُرَة السَّلَة

I play basketball

أنا أَسْكُنُ في المَدِينَة الجَامِعِـيَّة

I live in the Dorm (university city)

أنا أَدْرُسُ اللُّغَة العَــرَبِيَّة

I study the Arabic language.

Activity 1: Choose the proper word that complete the meaning of each of the following sentences:

المَدينَـة – هَذا – أَنا – أَلْعبُ – وِلايَة – أدْرُسُ - هَذِهِ - أُسْرَتِي

1. .... بَيْتٌ كَبيرٌ

2. ....طالِـبٌ في الجامِعَة

3. أنا .... اللُّغَةَ الإسْبانِـيـَّة

4. أنا .... الكُرَة في الحَدِيقَة

5. أنا مِنْ .... كُولورادو

6. .... كَـبـيـرَة جِداً

7. .... مَـكْـتَـبَـة الجامِعَة

8. أنا أَسْكنُ فِي .... الجَامِعِيـَّة.

Introducing Yourself

Dialogue 4: Greeting

طارِق: مَرْحَباً

بُـثـَيـْنـَة: أهْلاً وَ سَهْلاً

طارق: أَنا اِسمي طارِق، وَ أَنْتِ؟

بثينة: أَنا اِسمي بُـثــَيـْنـَة.

طارِق: أهْلاً وَ سَهْلاً، تَـشَـرَّفْـنـا.

Tarek: Hello,. Bothaina: Hello., Tarek: My name is Tarek, and you?, Bothaina: My name is Bothaina., Tarek: Welcome and honored

Activity 2: Re- Write dialogue 4

Dialogue 5: Greeting

بُثـيْـنَة		صَباحُ الخَـيْـرِ يا طارِق؟

طارِق:		صَباحُ الخَـيْـرِ يا بُثـيْـنَة.

بُثـيْـنَة		مَنْ هَذا يا طارِق؟

طارِق:		هَذا هُوَ الأُسْتَاذُ هَيْثَم، و هُوَ مغربـيٌّ

بُثـيْـنَة		وَمَنْ هَذِهِ يـا طارِق ؟

طارِق		هَذِهِ هِيَ الأُسْتاذةُ وَفاء، وَ هِيَ مَغْرِبِـيَّـةٌ أَيْضـاً.

Good morning Tarek., Good Morning Bothainah, who is this Tarek?, This professor Haitham and he is Moroccan., And who is this?, This is professor Wafaa, and she is Moroccan Too,

---

Activity 3: Re- Write dialogue 5

Dialogue 6: Where do you live?

مارْك أنا أَسْكُنُ في مَدِينَة "رينو"، و أَنْتَ يا چُـون؟

چُـون أنَا أَسْكُنُ في مَدِينَة "سباركْس".

مارك هَـلْ هِيَ قـرِيبَة مِنْ مَدِينَة "رينو"؟

چـون نعم، هي قَـرِيبَة جِداً.

I live in the city of Reno. And you John?, I live in the city of Sparks., Is it near the city of Reno., Yes, it is very near.

Activity 4: Write dialogue 6

Dialogue 5 & 6 Vocabulary

Who	مَنْ
The professor	الأُسْتَاذُ
Moroccan (m)	مغربــيٌّ
I reside	أَسْكُنُ
City	مَدِينَة
near	قــرِيبَة
very	جِداً
Yes	نَعَمْ

Activity 5 : create a short paragraph about yourself in no less than five sentences.

Hamza in the Middle and at the End of the Word

In this lesson we will learn about the hamza in the middle and final positions. First, we need to refresh our mind with the three short vowels and the sukuun: ـْ ـُ ـِ ـَ

The sukun and the three short vowels have relative "seniority" compared to each other.

The order of strength is:

1) Kasrah 2) Dammahh 3) FaTha 4) Sukun.

The chart below, is illustrating the strength of the short vowels and sukuun and the seats for the hamza in each case.

1st Strongest	2nd Strongest	3rd Strongest	Weakest	
ـِ	ـُ	ـَ	ـْ	The short vowel or sukuun that is associated with the hamza.
ـئـ / ئ	ؤ	أ	The seat *depends on* the vowel that precedes it	How the seat for the hamza should look like.

The rule is: The *seat for the hamza* is decided based on which short vowel is strongest, the short vowel of the letter that precedes the **Hamza** or the short vowel that accompanies the Hamza, whichever is ***stronger***.

The rule for reading the hamza in these case is: IGNORE the seat, because it is just an orthographic convention in the spelling of the word.

Examples					
To Be asked	سُئِلَ		لَ	ءِ	سُ
Question	سُؤَال	لْ	ا	ءَ	سُ
Calm	هَادِئْ	ءْ	دِ	ا	هَـ
Started	بَدَأَ		ءَ	دَ	بَ
Asked	سَأَلَ		لَ	ءَ	سَ

ACTIVITY 1: These words in the table below are missing the proper seated of the Hamzah. Find the proper seat according to the given short vowels.

	ؤ - ئـ - أ		
فـ ـَ ر	مسا ـِ ل	مِـ ـَـة	با ـِ س
ر ـَ ف	تتـ ـَ لم	يُـ ـْ من	يَـ ـْ كل

ACTIVITY 2: Listen to 12 words missing the seat of the Hamza. Listen and find the correct seat.

هَادِ...	مَيْـ وس	با ـــ س	تَـ لَم	بُـــ س	سُـــ ال
سُـ ـل	لِـــ ـلا	سَـــ م	مَسا ـل	مِـــ ات	فِـــ ران

Independent Hamza ء

The Hamzah could also be written independently on the line, *without any seat*.
This case occurs in multiple situations:

1) In the ***middle*** or at the ***end*** of a word, ***after*** the long vowels : ا & و

غِناءٌ	مَساءٌ
Singing	Evening
وُضوءٌ	مُروءَةٌ
Ablution	Virility

2) At the ***end*** of a word, ***after*** the long vowel: ي

مُسِيءٌ	بَطِيءٌ	قَمِيءٌ
harmful	slow	Disgusting

3) At the ***end*** of the word, if it is ***preceded*** by a letter voweled with ***sukuun***:

عِبْءٌ	جُزْءٌ	دِفْءٌ	شَيْءٌ	ضَوْءٌ
Burden	Part	Warmth	Thing	Light

Alif Maqsura

Alif maqsura means: shortened Alif. It is a long vowel ا which appears at the end of a word, however it is represented by this letter ى , this is a ي with no dots.

This letter is always pronounced as an Alif ا when it occurs in: names, some nouns, in some adjectives, and in some verbs.

> **Note**: In *most* nouns, the Alif maqsura is feminine marker sign as the Taa Marbouta ة.

Examples							
* مـوسَى	نـدَى	مُنَى	سَلْمَى	أَرْوَى	هُـدى	سَـلوَى	**Names**
* فـتـى	* مَأْوى	إلى	حـتَّـى	مَـتَـى	قُـرَى	مُوسِيقَى	**Nouns**
Young man	Shelter	To	Until	When	Villages	Music	
		فَـنَـى	جَـرَى	اِشْتَـرَى	رَوَى	بَنَى	**Verbs**
		To perish	To run	To buy	To water	To build	
Note: * Masculine.							

Read the following sentences with the help of your teacher, guess the meaning of the highlighted words, and then write their English equivalents next to each Arabic sentence.

أنا أُحِـبُّ المُوسِـيقَى	**Love**
سَـلْمَى أُخْـتي الكُـبْـرَى	Eldest
*مُـوسَـى جَـرَى في الحَدِيـقَـة	Ran
أنا طَالِبٌ فِي الكُـلِّـيَـة	College
أَبـــي طَـبِـيـبٌ	Physician
أُمــي مُـهَـنْـدِسَـةٌ	Engineer
أنا أَذْهَبُ إِلى الجَامِعَةِ بِسَـيَّـارَتِـي	To Go
هذا بَـيْـتٌ جَدِيدٌ	New

هذا بَيْتٌ قَدِيمٌ Old

هَذِهِ زَوْجَتِي My Wife

أَنَا أُحِبُّ جَدَّتِي جِداً My Grandmother

عِنْدي أَخٌ وَ أُخْتٌ Sister/ Brother

أنا أُحِبُّ البُرْتُقال وَ الفَرَاوْلَة Orange / strawberry

هَذِه حَافِلَةٌ كَبِيرَةٌ وَ جَدِيدَةٌ Bus

نافِذَةُ الصَّفِ كَبِيرَةٌ Window/ Classroom

Activity 6: Write the 12 previous sentences in the table below.

.1
.2
.3
.4
.5
.6
.7
.8
.9
.10
.11
.12

Activity 7: Dictation: Your teacher will dictate you some of the new words.

.2	.1
.4	.3
.6	.5
.8	.7
.10	.9
.12	.11
.14	.13
.16	.15
.18	.17
.20	.19

The Arabic Numbers 1 -10

Following are the numerals in Arabic from **<u>Zero to Ten</u>**, Masculine and feminine:

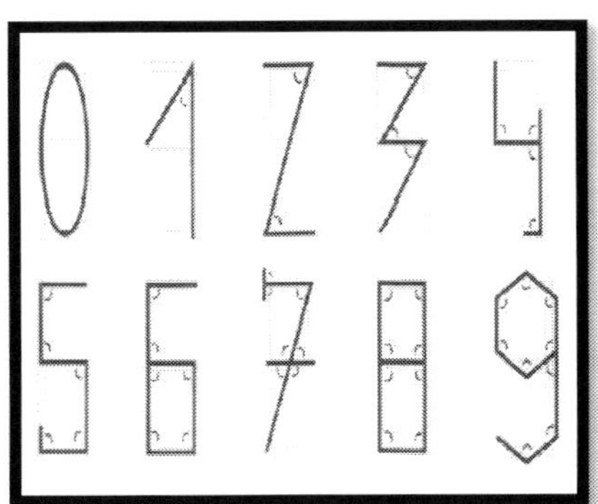

Note: These are the original Arabic numbers, what we use in Arabic are the Indian numbers.

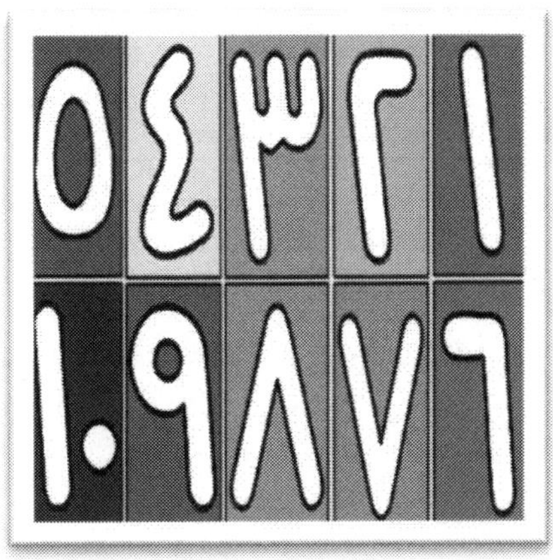

F.	M.	
صِفْر	صِفْر	**0**
وَاحِـدَة	وَاحِدٌ	1.
اِثْـنَـتَـانِ	اِثْـنَـانِ	2.
ثَـلاثَـة	ثَـلاثْ	3.
أَرْبَـعَـة	أَرْبَـعْ	4.
خَـمْـسَـة	خَـمْـس	5.
سِـتَّـة	سِـتّْ	6.
سَـبْـعَـة	سَبْـعْ	7.
ثَـمَـانِـيَـة	ثَـمَـانْ	8.
تِـسْـعَـة	تِـسْعْ	9.
عَـشَـرَة	عَـشَـرْ	10.

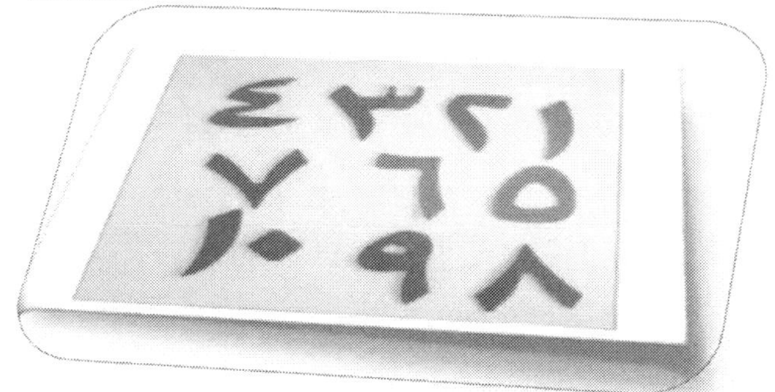

Activity 8: Listen to the following numbers and write the English equivalent in the table provided

5)	4)	3)	2)	1)
10)	9)	8)	7)	6)
15)	14)	13)	12)	11)

Activity 9: Listen to the following numbers and write the number you hear in Arabic in the table provided.

.5	.4	.3	.2	.1
.10	.9	.8	.7	.6
.15	.14	.13	.12	.11

Activity 10: Listen to the following numbers and write the English equivalent in the table provided

.5	.4	.3	.2	.1
.10	.9	.8	.7	.6
.15	.14	.13	.12	.11
.20	.19	.18	.17	.16
.25	.24	.23	.22	.21

ACTIVITY 11: Listen to the following numbers and write the number you hear in Arabic in the table provided.

5.	4.	3.	2.	1.
10.	9.	8.	7.	6.
15.	14.	13.	12.	11.
20.	19.	18.	17.	16.

Here & There

هُـنا

هُـناكَ

The Interrogative Question: How Many?

The question word كَـمْ is used to express the question" how many".

Note: كم is always followed by an ***indefinite, singular noun***.

This noun ending case should be ***FaTha*** and tanween could be applied.

كَـــمْ طالباً في الصَّفِ؟

في الصَّف تِسْعْ.

كَـــمْ شجرةً هُـناك ؟

هناك سَـبْعْ.

Activity 12: Create a question and an answer for each picture in the table below, the first one is done for you.

	– كم قلماً هناك؟ – هُـناكَ سِتٌّ
	-- --
	-- --
	-- --
	-- --

Days of the week أَيَّامُ الأُسْبُوع

Sunday	الأَحَـــد
Monday	الإِثْـنَـيْـن
Tuesday	الـثُّـلاثـــاء
Wednesday	الأَرْبِــعـــاء
Thursday	الخَـمِـيـس
Friday	الجُـمُـعَـة
Saturday	الـسَّـبْـت

Activity 13: Answer the following questions in Arabic:

1. In What days do you have your Arabic class?

أذهبُ إلى صف اللغة العربية في يوم الإثنين و الثلاثاء و الأربعاء و الخميس.

2. What day do you go to the movie?

3. How many books are in your bag?

4. How many tables in here?

5. What days do you go to the university?

6. What days do you work? And when?

7. What do you like to play?

Lesson 7 Vocabulary List

1. Zero	صِفْر	25. My Grand Mother	جَدَّتي
2. One	وَاحِد	26. Strawberry	الفَـرَاوْلَة
3. Two	اِثْنَانِ	27. Orange	البُرْتـُـقَال
4. Three	ثَلاثْ	28. Window	نـافِـذَةٌ
5. Four	أَرْبَعْ	29. Here	هُـنا
6. Five	خَمْسْ	30. There	هُـناك
7. Six	سِتٌّ	31. My Wife	زَوْجَـتِـي
8. Seven	سَبْعْ	32. How many/ How much	كَـمْ
9. Eight	ثَمَانْ	33. Tree	شَـجَـرةٌ
10. Nine	تِسْعْ	34. Student	طالب
11. Ten	عَـشَرْ	35. Old	قَدِيـمٌ
12. Sunday	الأَحَد	36. New	جَدِيدٌ
13. Monday	الإِثْـنَـيْن	37. Physician	طَبِـيـبٌ
14. Tuesday	الثُّلاثَاء	38. College	الكُـلِّـيَـة
15. Wednesday	الأَرْبِعاء	39. The eldest	الكُـبْـرى
16. Thursday	الخَمِيس	40. The Music	المُوسِـيـقَى
17. Friday	الجُمْعَة	41. Who	مَنْ
18. Saturday	السَّبْـت	42. Moroccan (m)	مغربـيٌّ
19. To Start	بَدَأ	43. I reside	أَسْكُنُ
20. To Ask	سَأَلَ	44. City	مَدِينَة
21. Calm	هَادِئ	45. near	قَـرِيبَة
22. very	جِداً	46. To run	جَـرَى
23. Dorm	المَدِينَة الجَامِعِـيَّة	47. Yes	نَعَمْ
24. Basketball	كُرَة السَّلَة	48. State	ولاية

LESSON 8

The Colors الأَلْوان

We will introduce the colors through 2 groups:

A. The first group consists of 6 colors, which they share many aspects.

Look at the table below, can you figure them out? Your teacher will help you.

أَزْرَق Blue	أَخْـضَـرْ Green	أَحْـمَـرْ Red
أَسْـوَدْ Black	أَبْـيَـضْ White	أَصْـفَـرْ Yellow
*Color : لوْن		

Note: colors can be masculine or feminine as they agree with nouns in gender and number.
So here is the rule of switching the 6 colors of the first group to feminine:

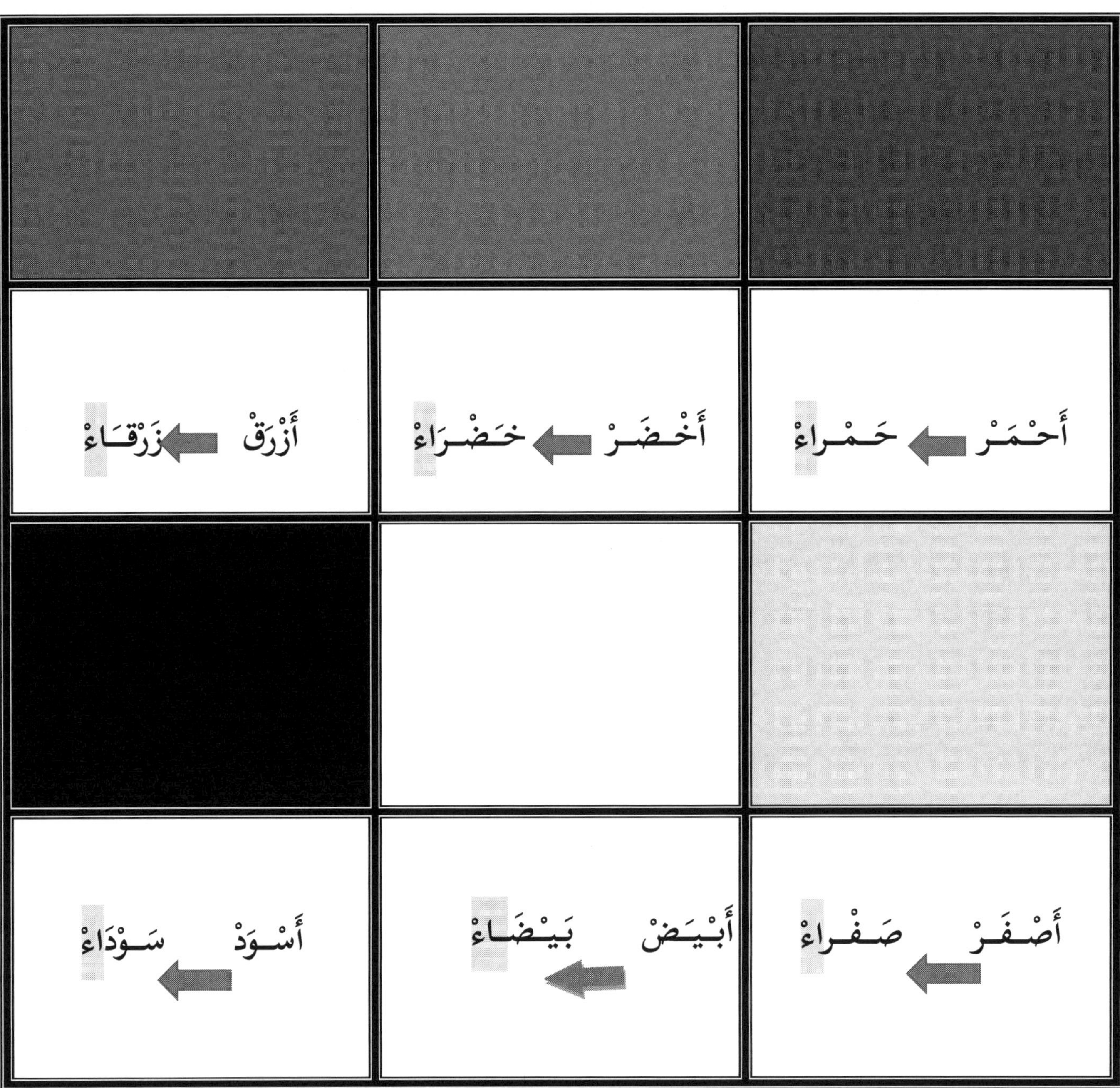

Activity 4: Read the following sentences and suggest the proper missing color (s) in Arabic.

1) أَسْكُنُ في البَيْت..............	
2) عِندي سَيَّارَة	
3) عَلَم فَرَنْسا ....و.............و........	
4) لَوْنُ بَيْتي ___	
5) مَعِي قَلَم ___	
6) لَوْن الـشَّمْسِ ___	

B. The second group of colors or any color other than the first 6 colors we learned,

The relative adjective يّ is used by adding it to some nouns to create adjectives of color.

Read the following with your teacher, figure out the color and create the feminine form as the given example.

Color in Feminine	Color in Masculine	Noun + relative يّ	Your Notes	
برتقاليَّة	برتقاليّ	بُرْتُقال + يّ		
		*وَرْدَة + يّ		
		*فِضَّة + يّ		
		رَمادْ + يّ		
		ذَهَبْ + يّ		
		بُـنْ+ يّ		
		بَنَـفْـسِج + يّ		

Note: In order to express shades of a color, we use the words:

غامِق =Dark / Deep, and the word فاتِح = Light

Activity 5: Write your own sentences describing some of the item surrounding you, using different colors in each description. Stretch your sentences to include vocabulary you have learned from previous lessons.

.1
.2
.3
.4
.5
.6
.7
.8

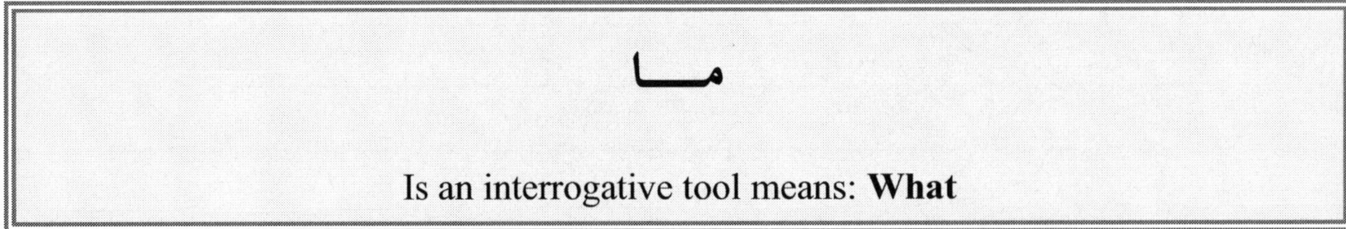

مـــا

Is an interrogative tool means: **What**

In order to ask about the color of anything, we need to use مـــا to firm the question.

Examples:

	لونُ السَّيَّارة أَحْمَر	ما لَوْنُ السَّيَّارةْ؟
	لون القَلَم أَزْرَق	ما لَوْنُ القَلَمْ؟

How about if we just use the color of an item in a regular sentence?
Pay attention to the color agreement with the noun:

	هَـذِهِ سَـيَّـارَةٌ حَـمْـراءٌ
	هَذا قَـلَـمٌ أَزْرَقٌ

Activity 6: Read the sentence below each picture displayed on the screen and write in the missing colors below. Be sure that the adjective agrees with the gender of the noun it describes. Check your answers with those of a classmate.

	إشَارَةُ المُرور ....و.......و.......	(1
	الحَافِلَةُ	(2
	لَوْنُ الكُرَة .... و	(3
	الكُرَةُ ....و...............	(4
	لَوْنُ الزَّهْرَة	(5
	لون العُـمْلة المَعْدِنـيَّة	(6
	السماء.......... و لونُ السحابِ	(7

Dialogue 7: Requesting a Pen

إِبْراهيم: يا چُون، هَلْ مَـعَـكَ قَـلَـمْ أَحْمَرْ؟

چـون: نَعَم، تَـفَـضَّـلْ القَـلَـمْ.

إبراهيم شُكْـراً.

چـون عَـفْـواً.

Hey John: Do you have a pen? Yes, (favorably accept) the pen., Thanks., Welcome.

Communication Skills: Practice with your partner, switch roles 4 times, then take turns and practice with another pair.

AActivity7: Re-write Dialogue 7

أَشْكَال Shapes

Start reading the shapes in Arabic with a class partner, then write a sentence below each shape. The first one is done for you.

هذا شَكْل دائِرَة / هَذِهِ دائرة بُرْتقالِيَّة

هِـلال

The Attached Pronouns الضَّمائِر المُـتَّـصِلَـة

Object pronouns (me, you, us, him, her, them) are used when you do something directly to someone or something else. When we attach pronoun suffixes to nouns, we are indicating who possesses. In Arabic, we have one set of letters that we use, however,

- When attached to nouns, it indicates possession (**possessive pronouns**) and is suffixed to nouns,
- When attached to verbs, it indicates the **object of a verb.**
- Also, it could be attached to **preposition**.

Although the first two usages are being exactly the same, however, they are different in their distribution and in their meanings.
Today, we will learn only their usages as possessives for the singular pronouns.

Look at the table below and practice with your teacher.

Examples:	Possessive Pronoun	Independent Pronoun	
كِـتابـي	ي	أَنـا	I
كِـتابُـكَ	كَ	أَنْـتَ	You M.
كِـتابُـكِ	كِ	أَنْـتِ	You F.
كِـتـابُـهُ	ـهُ	هُـوَ	He
كِـتـابُـهـا	هَـا	هِـيَ	She
كتابنَا	نَا	نَحْنُ	We
كتابكُم	كُم	أنْتُم	You All
كتابكُن	كُنَّ	أنْتُنَّ	You All F.
كتابهُم	هُم	هُم	They
كتابهُن	هُنَّ	هُنَّ	They F.
كتابكما	كما	أنتما	You Two
كتابهما	هما	هما	They Both

Activity 8: The following nouns are attached with the possessive ي , attach these nouns to a different possessive pronoun of your choice in the opposite column. Check your answers with your teacher and classmates.

	Noun + Attached pronouns	The noun
Her mother	أُمُّــــــها	.1 أُمْـ
		.2 بَـيْـت
		.3 مُعَـلِّمَة
		.4 أُسْـتاذ
		.5 جَامِعَـة
		.6 قَـلَمْ
		.7 سَـيَّارَة
		.8 كُرَّاسَة
		.9 مَـكْـتَـبْ
		.10 حَاسوب

Activity 9: Replace the highlighted word in each sentence with the proper attached pronoun.

	1) هَذِهِ كُرَّاسَة أُخْتي
	2) هذه حَقيبَة مُدَرِسَتُها
	3) هذه سَيارة أُمي
	4) هَذَا مَكْتَب المُعلِم
	5) هذا بَيْت جَدَّتِي
	6) هذا حَاسوب أَخي
	7) هذا مُعلِّم أَخي
	8) هذه جامِعَة أُخْتي
	9) هذا مُديـر أَبي **manager**
	10) هذا مَطار المَدينَة **airport**

Dialogue 8: Getting Acquainted

يُوسُفْ	: مَرْحباً يا زَهْـرَة، [1]مَنْ مَعَكِ؟
زَهْرَة	: هذا [2]اِبْني فادي.
يُوسُف	: أهلاً فادي، هلْ أنْتَ [3]طالِبٌ؟
فادي	: نَعَم، أنا طالِبٌ في المَدْرَسَةِ [4]الثَّانَـوِيَّة
يوسُف	: أَهْلاً يا فادي، [5]تَـشَـرَّفْـنا.
فادي	: أَهْلاً بِـكَ، تَـشَـرَّفْـنا.

[1] Who is with you?, [2] My son., [3] Student., [4] Secondary school., [5] Honored

Communication Skills: Practice with your partner, switch roles 4 times, then take turns and practice with another pair.

Activity 10: Write dialogue 8

Activity 11: Fill in the blank with the appropriate words:

1. عندي سيارة ....

2. أسكن في بيت جدي ....

3. علَم أمريكا أبيض و .... و أزرق.

1. لون الشمس.....................

4. هذه العملة المعدنية ....

5. ابن أختي، طالب، في المدرسة ....

6. كراسة اللغة العربية ....

7. سهمُ الإشارة ....

8. في السَّماء، نجمة كبيرة و لونها............

9. .... في السماء اليَوْم.

10. كتابي في الحقيبة ....

11. معي قلم .... و قلم ....

12. غرفتي .... الشكل.

Lesson 8 Vocabulary List

1. Circle	دائِـرَة	1. Red (M & F)	أحْـمَـرْ / حَـمْـراءْ
2. Triangle	مُـثَـلَّث	2. Green (M & F)	أخْـضَـرْ / خَـضْـرَاءْ
3. Square	مُرَبَّع	3. Yellow (M & F)	أصْـفَـرْ / صَـفْـراءْ
4. Rectangle	مُسْـتَطيل	4. White (M & F)	أبْـيَـضْ/ بَـيْـضَـاءْ
5. Cube	مُـكَعَّب	5. Blue (M & F)	أزْرَق / زَرْقَـاءْ
6. Rhombus	مُعَـيَّن	7. Black (M & F)	أسْـوَدْ / سَـوْدَاءْ
6. Arrow	سَهْم	8. Color	لَـوْن
7. Heart	قَـلْب	9. Flag	عَلَم
8. Star	نَجْمَة	10. Orange color	بُرْتُـقاليّ
9. Cross	صَلِـيب	11. Rose Color	وَرْدِيّ
10. Crescent	هِلال	12. Gray	رَمادِيّ
11. Computer	حاسوب	13. Golden color	ذَهَبِيّ
12. Manager	مُدير	14. Brown color	بُـنِيّ

13. Airport	مَطار	15. Purple Color	بَـنَـفْـسِـجِـيّ
14. School	مَدْرَسَـة	16. Traffic Light	إشارَة المُرور
15. Secondary	الـثّـانَوِيَّة	17. Bus	الحافِـلة
16. Honored	تَـشَـرْفْـنـا	18. Flower	زَهْرَة
17. Son/ Daughter	اِبْن / ة	19. Who	مَنْ
18. The sky	السَّماء	20. The currency	العُـمْلة
19. The clouds	السَّحاب	21. Metallic	مَعْدَنِيـَّة
20. Dark in shades	غامِق	22. Light in shades	فاتِح

LESSON 9

Verbs System in Arabic Language

There are two essential moods/tenses in Arabic.

- The past (الماضي) - used to indicate actions that have been completed. This conjugation involves adding suffixes to the "base" form of the verb.
- The present (المضارع) - used to indicate actions that have not been completed yet. This conjugation requires the addition of prefixes and, in some cases, suffixes as well.

Note: There are <u>no infinitive forms</u> of verbs in Arabic. Instead, typically <u>the masculine third-person perfect</u> form is used. كتب- درس- ذهب

There are two main classes of verbs in Arabic: sound (صحيح) and weak (معتل).
An outline of the types of verbs in MSA:

1) **Sound verbs الفعل الصحيح**- don't have a و or ي as one of the three root letters

2) **Geminate/doubled verbs الفعل المضعف** - where the second and third radicals of the root are the same
3) **Hamzated verbs الفعل المهموز** - where ء is one of the consonants
4) **Weak verbs الفعل المعتل**- have a و or ي as one or more of the root radicals
   i. **Assimilated verbs الفعل المثال**- begin with و or ي (usually و); in the present and in other situations the و often disappears
   ii. **Hollow verbs الفعل الأجوف** - the second radical is either a و or ي ; in the past, the و or ي is replaced by an ا
   iii. **Defective verbs الفعل الناقص**- where the final root radical is either و or ي a

Note: In this lesson we will learn the sound verbs conjugation (past and present) for the pronouns that we learned in previous lessons. Look at the table below and repeat with your teacher.

Verb: To Do // فَـعَـلَ //

Present المضارع	Past الماضي	Pronouns الضمائر	
أَفْـعَـلُ	فَـعَـلْـتُ	أَنا	I
تَـــفْـعَـلُ	فَعَلــْـتَ	أَنْتَ	You M.
تَـــفْـعَـلِـــيـــنَ	فَـعَـلْــتِ	أَنْتِ	You F.
يَـــفْـعَـلُ	فَـعَـلَ	هُوَ	He
تَـــفْـعَـلُ	فَـعَـلَــتْ	هِيَ	She
تَفْعَلَانِ	فَعَلْتُمَا	أنتما	You two M
تَفْعَلَانِ	فَعَلْتُمَا	أنتما	You two F
يَفْعَلَانِ	فَعَلَا	هما	They Both M
تَفْعَلَانِ	فَعَلَتَا	هما	They Both F.
نَفْعَلُ	فَعَلْنَا	نحن	We
تَفْعَلُونَ	فَعَلْتُم	أنتم	You All
تَفْعَلْنَ	فَعَلْتُنَّ	أنتن	You All F.
يَفْعَلُونَ	فَعَلُوا	هم	They
يَفْعَلْنَ	فَعَلْنَ	هن	They F.

Below is a list of sound verbs that will conjugate exactly as verb فعل. These verbs are frequently used in our daily lives.

Learn New Vocabulary					
Group 1		**Group 2**		**Group 3**	
Go	ذهب .1	Make	صنع .1	Accept	قبِل .1
Succeed	نجح .2	Mean	قصد .2	Advise	نصح .2
Guarded	حرس .3	Obtain	حصل .3	Allow	سمح .3
Hit	ضرب .4	Open	فتح .4	Appear	ظهر .4
Hurt	جرح .5	Laugh	ضحك .5	Attach/ Connect	ربط .5
Joke	مزح .6	Plant	زرع .6	Bake	خبز .6
Jump	قفز .7	Play	لعب .7	Bleed	نزف .7
Draw	رسم .8	Prevent	منع .8	Blow	نفخ .8
Know	عرِف .9	Drink	شرِب .9	Break	كسر .9
Do	فعل .10	Sweep	مسح .10	Burn	حرق .10

ACTIVITY 1: Use the form below to practice conjugation

Conjugate of the verb _____ ______

المضارع **Present**	المــاضــي **Past**	الضمير **Pronoun**
		أَنــا
		أَنْتَ
		أنْــتِ
		هُــوَ
		هِــيَ

Conjugate of the verb _____ ______

المضارع **Present**	المــاضــي **Past**	الضمير **Pronoun**
		أَنــا
		أَنْتَ
		أنْــتِ
		هُــوَ
		هِــيَ

Conjugate of the verb ______ _______

المضارع Present	الماضي Past	الضمير Pronoun
		أَنـا
		أنْتَ
		أنْـتِ
		هُـوَ
		هِـيَ

Conjugate of the verb ______ _______

المضارع Present	الماضي Past	الضمير Pronoun
		أَنـا
		أنْتَ
		أنْـتِ
		هُـوَ
		هِـيَ

Conjugate of the verb _____ ______

المضارع Present	المــاضـــي Past	الضمير Pronoun
		أَنــا
		أَنْتَ
		أَنْــتِ
		هُــوَ
		هِــيَ

Conjugate of the verb _____ ______

المضارع Present	المــاضـــي Past	الضمير Pronoun
		أَنــا
		أَنْتَ
		أَنْــتِ
		هُــوَ
		هِــيَ

Conjugate of the verb _____ ______

المضارع Present	المــاضــي Past	الضمير Pronoun
		أَنــا
		أَنْتَ
		أَنْــتِ
		هُــوَ
		هِــيَ

Conjugate of the verb _____ ______

المضارع Present	المــاضــي Past	الضمير Pronoun
		أَنــا
		أَنْتَ
		أَنْــتِ
		هُــوَ
		هِــيَ

Future Tense

Note: In Arabic, the future tense of a verb is the present conjugation + the letter س as a prefix.
Example: [Present أنا أذهبُ] [Future أنا سأذهبُ]

Verb: To Do // فَـعَـلَ //		
Future المستقبل	**Pronouns الضمائر**	
سأَفْـعَـلُ	أَنا	**I**
ستَـفْـعَـلُ	أَنْتَ	**You M.**
ستَفْـعَـلِـينَ	أَنْتِ	**You F.**
سيَـفْـعَـلُ	هُوَ	**He**
ستَـفْـعَـلُ	هِيَ	**She**
ستَفْعَلَانِ	أنتما	You Two M.
ستَفْعَلَانِ	أنتما	You Two F.
سيَفْعَلَانِ	هما	They Both M.
ستَفْعَلَانِ	هما	They Both F
سنَفْعَلُ	نحن	We
ستَفْعَلُونَ	أنتم	You All
ستَفْعَلْنَ	أنتن	You All F.
سيَفْعَلُونَ	هم	They
سيَفْعَلْنَ	هن	They F.

Activity 1: Conjugate the verbs between parentheses in past, present and future tense according to the associated personal pronoun, in the given space. Mark the case ending of each conjugation form:

Future	Past	Present	Verb in infinitive form + Pronoun
			أنا + (ربط)
			هي + (فعل)
			أنتَ + (ظهر)
			هُوِ + (جرح)
			أنتِ + (قفز)
			هِي + (منع)

Activity2: Conjugate the verbs between parentheses in the given space. Mark the case ending of each conjugation form:

1.	أبي__________________ (زرع) شجرة برتقال في الحديقة (past)
2.	أمي__________________ (خبز) في الصباح (past)
3.	الشمس __________________ (ظهر) في الصباح (present)
4.	أختي __________________ (جرح) يدها (past)
5.	الولد __________________ (قفز) من على الطاولة (present)
6.	الولد __________________ (رسم) صورة جميلة (present)
7.	الولد و البنت __________________ (شرب) عصير الفراولة (present)
8.	العامل __________________ (مسح) الطاولة (past)
9.	أنا __________________ (حرق) يدي (past)
10.	أنتِ __________________ (نجح) في اللغة العربية (past)
11.	الطالِبتانِ __________________ (عرف) هذا الأستاذ (present)
12.	الولدان __________________ (فتح) الحقيبة الكبيرة (past)
13.	الأُمَّانِ __________________ (نفخ) البالونات (present)
14.	الولد و البنت __________________ (زرع) الورد في الحديقة (present)
15.	البنتان __________________ (لعب) كرة السلة (present)
16.	أبي __________________ (فتح) باب الغرفة (past)
17.	الأستاذان __________________ (نصح) الطالِب (present)
18.	الأستاذان __________________ (لعب) مع الطالبانِ (past)
19.	الولد __________________ (كسر) القلم (past)
20.	هذا الولد __________________ (ضرب) هذا الولد (past)

Dialogue 9: Chatting with a Friend over the weekend

أَيْمَنْ أَيْنَ سَـتَـذْهَـبُ فِي عُـطْـلَة نِهايَة الأُسْبُوع يا أَمْجَـد؟

أَمْجَـد سَأَذْهَـبُ إلى السِّـينِما، هَـلْ تَـذْهبُ مَعِي؟

أيمن فِي أَيِّ يَوْم؟

أمجد فِي يَوْم السَّـبْت.

أيمن لا، آسِـف أَنا مَـشْغُول جِداً يَوْم السَّبْت.
هل تَـذْهَـبُ مَعي إِلىَ السِّينِما يَوْم الأَحَد؟

أَمْجَد نَعَـم، سَأَذْهبُ مَعَـكَ يَوْم الأَحَدْ.

أَيْمَن مُمْتاز.

Communication Skill: practice with your teachers and roleplay with your class partner at least 6 times.

Dialogue 10 Vocabulary

1. End	نِهايَة	7. In	فِـي
2. To Go	ذهب / تَـذْهبُ	8. Vacation	عُـطْـلَة
3. Day	يَوْم	9. Week	الأُسْبُوع
4. Sorry	آسِـف	10. Excellent	مُمْتاز
5. Very	جِداً	11. Busy	مَـشْغُـول
6. Yes	نَعَـم	12. No	لا

Write The Dialogue

Question words

Would you / Do you / is it / Could you ..	هَــلْ
Who	مَــنْ
How	كَـيْـفَ
What + noun	مَــا
What + Verb	مَــاذا
Where	أَيْــنَ
How much? Or How many?	كَــمْ
When	مَــتــَى
Why	لِــمــاذا
Which	أَيْ
Whose	لِمَــنْ

Note: you have learned some of these question words in previous dialogue.
This useful table has them all for your future reference.

ACTIVITY 3: Create questions for the following sentences, the first two are done for you. Check your answers with your classmates.

.1 القَلَم مَعي	أَيْنَ القلم ؟
.2 نَعم، عِنْدي سيارة	هَلْ عِنْدكَ سيَّارة؟
.3 اِسْمي أحْمد.	
.4 أنا أُحِـبُ جَـدي و جَدَتي	
.5 هذا القَلم أزْرَق	
.6 أذْهَـبُ إلىَ الجامِعَة بالسَّيارة	
.7 عِندي حاسوب فِي البيْت	
.8 نعم، عِنْدي أُخْتٌ واحِدَة	
.9 سأذْهَـب غَـداً إلى الـسِّـينـما	
.10 أُحِـبُ القِراءَة	

Activty 4: Create a question for each of the following sentences. You may use any word you learned to create these questions, be creative. Use the same process we learn in class on a draft paper:

نعم، عندي سيارة

سأذهب إلى المدرسة في الصباح

أبي سيذهب إلى السينما يوم السبت

نعم، اليوم، أنا مشغول جداً مع أسرتي

في الأسبوع، سبعة أيام

هُما بخير و الحمدُ لله

سأذهب غداً مع أخي إلى الحديقة

عندي حاسوبانِ اثنان في البيت

معي خمسة أقلام في حقيبتي

عندي أخ واحِد و أُخت واحِدة

Activity 5: Read the following paragraph then translate it in the space provided:

أنا طالِبٌ فــي الجامِعَة، فــي كُليَّة اللُّغات.

أنا مِن مَدِينَة " دالاس" بِولايَة "تِكساس" .

أَسْكُن في المَدينَة الجامِعِـيَّة مَعَ صَديقي "چون". عِندي سَيَّارة بَنَفْسِجية.

فــي يَوْم الأَرْبعاء أَذْهبُ إلــى الجامِعة مَع صديقي بِسَيَّارَتِه الذَهبيَّة.

و فــي يَوْم الجُمُعة أذهبُ إلــى الجامعة بالحافِلة الكَبيرة.

في حَقيبَتي أرْبَعَة أقْلام و ثَلاثَة كُتب و كُرَّاسة واحِدَة.

أنا أحبُ اللَّون الأَصْفَر و الأَزْرَق.

صَديقي عِنْدَهُ صَديقَة مِن لُبنان. و أنا عندي صديق يابانيّ.

أُمي طَبيَة و أبــي أُستاذ في جامِعة " كاليفورنيا"، مَكْتَب أبي كبير .

عِندي أخ و أُخت. أُسْرتي عِندها بَيْت كَبير لَونه أَبْيَض و فِيهِ حَديقَة كَبيرة و جَميلة.

الحَديقة فِيها وَرْد و فَراشات. البَيْت قَريب مِن مَطار المَدينَة.

أنا أُحِبُّ المُوسيقَى الكَلاسِيكِيَّة. جَدَّتــي عِندها نَافِذة كَبيرة في بَيَتها و مزرعة فيها فراولة و بطيخ و برتقال. في يوم السَّبْت أَلعبُ كُرَة السَّلة مَع صَديقي "مارْك".

Case Ending In Arabic Language

In Arabic, case endings are short vowel markings, in most cases, that are related to the ends of words to designate the words' grammatical function. This is not a character in English and similar languages.

Example: if a word is the subject of a sentence, we use a special case ending to indicate that; if a word is the object of a verb, we use different case ending to designate that, etc..

This process requires a competent knowledge of Arabic grammar, however , at this point, only your awareness of this case is needed.

Usually, case endings are not written except in certain texts like the holy books and children' books.

Step by step, we will learn together the case system. Below is a table that shows the difference between them:

The Different Ending Cases For Singular Nouns	
Nominative Case مرفوع	The nominative case, also called the subjective, marks the subject of a phrase. Example: الطَّــالِبــةُ في الصفِ الكَبيرِ The subject is the noun (or pronoun) that performs the action of the verb. The Nominative Case of singular nouns is the __ُ__ Dammah over the last letter of the noun, whether it is a masculine or feminine, as we see in the word الطالبةُ.
Accusative Case منصوب	The accusative case deals mostly, with the direct objects of verbs. Example : "I drink coffee"// أنا أشربُ القهوةَ The direct object is "coffee", and thus it is in the accusative case. Thus, the case ending must be __َ FaTha for the singular nouns, whether it is a masculine or feminine.
Genitive Case مجرور	The genitive case deals mostly with nouns and adjectives that occur after prepositions and other constructions that we will study in the future. Example: الطالبُ في الصَّـفِ // "The student is in the classroom " The word " classroom" is preceded by a preposition, thus the case ending must be __ِ below the last letter, whether it is a masculine or feminine.

The Dual الْـمُـثَـنْـى

In this lesson we will learn the following:

- The dual form (الْمُثَـنَّـى) of the Arabic Nouns, which is the form that relates to two of something.
- We will also learn the dual form of the Demonstrative Pronouns for the near objects for both the masculine and the feminine objects (i.e. these and those):

In Arabic, nouns fall into three categories as follows:

1. Singular - which relates to a single noun
2. Dual - which indicates two of something
3. Plural - which indicates more than two of something (Will learn the plural in a later lesson)

The table below will show the different categories of noun:

English	Arabic	Masc. / Fem.
1. The (m) teacher (Singular) الْمُفْرَدُ	الْمُدَرِّسُ	الْمُذَكَّرُ (Masc.)
2. Two (m) teachers (Dual) الْمُثَنَّى	الْمُدَرِّسَانِ	
3. The (m) teachers (Plural) الْجَمْعُ	الْمُدَرِّسُونَ	
4. The (f) teacher (Singular) الْمُفْرَدُ	الْمُدَرِّسَةُ	الْمُؤَنَّثُ (Fem.)
5. Two (f) teachers (Dual) الْمُثَنَّى	الْمُدَرِّسَتَانِ	
6. The (f) teachers (Plural) الْجَمْعُ	الْمُدَرِّسَاتُ	

In order to change a singular Arabic noun to the Dual, you need to follow these steps:

A. Nominative Case:

For Singular Masculine Noun:

1) The **last letter** of the word has its vowel **replaced** with a single **fatha**.

2) The suffix of انِ is added to the word and Kasrah is added to the Noun.

Examples:

	Dual M.	Singular M.
2 Students	طَالِـبَـانِ	طَالِبٌ
2 pens	قلمانِ	قَلَمٌ
2 keys	مِفْتاحانِ	مِفْتاحٌ
2 sons	اِبْنانِ	اِبْنٌ
2 weeks	أسْبوعانِ	أسْبوعٌ
2 days	يومانِ	يَوْمٌ

<u>For Singular Feminine Noun:</u>

1) The last letter ة is changed to the letter ت

2) The last letter (which is now) ت has its **vowel** <u>replaced</u> with a single **fatħah** regardless of its existing vowel.

3) The suffix of انِ is added to the word, and Kasrah is added to the Noun.

Examples:

	Dual F.	Singular F.
2 F. students	طَالِـبَتَـانِ	طَالِبَةٌ
2 cars	سَـيَّارَتَـانِ	سَـيَّارة
2 boards	سَـبُّورتَـانِ	سَـبُّورَة
2 mothers	أُمـَّـانِ	أُمٌّ
2 girls	بِـنْـتَـانِ	بِنْتٌ
2 tables	طـاوِلَـتَـانِ	طاوِلَةٌ

B. In the Genitive and Accusative Case:

For Singular Masculine Noun:

1. A single **Fatĥah** is added on **the last letter**.
2. The suffix يْنِ , Kasrah is added to the Noun.

Examples:

Dual masculine noun	Singular masculine noun:
الطالبانِ مَعَ المُدَرِّسَيْنِ	1. الطالبُ مَعَ المُدَرِّسِ
The 2 students are with the 2 teachers	Students is with the teacher
أنا عِنْدَ الْمُدَرِّسَيْنِ	2. أنا عِنْدَ الْمُدَرِّسِ
I am at the 2 teachers	I am at the teacher
أكل الولدُ التُّفاحَتَيْن	3. أَكَلَ الوَلَدُ التُّفاحَةَ
The boy ate the 2 apples	The boy ate the apple
أكلت البنتُ البُرْتُقالتيْن	4. أكلتْ البِنت البُرتقالةَ
The girl ate the 2 oranges	The girl ate the orange

For Singular Feminine Noun:

1. The last letter ة is changed to the letter ت
2. A **single fatĥah** is added over **the last letter** of the word.
3. The suffix يْنِ , is added to the Noun.

Examples

Dual feminine noun	Singular feminine noun
الكتابانِ فِي الحَقِيبَتَيْنِ	.1 الكِـتابُ فِي الحَقِيبَةِ
The 2 books are in the 2 bags	**The book is the bag**
العُصْفورانِ فَوْقَ الشَّجَرَتَيْنِ	.2 العُصْفورُ فَوْقَ الشَّجَرَةِ
The 2 sparows are on top of the 2 trees	The saprow is on the tree
البِنْتـانِ مَعَ المُدَرِّسَتَيْنِ.	.3 البِنْتـانِ مَعَ المُدَرِّسَةِ.
The 2 girls are with the 2 teachers	The 2 girls are with the teacher

In conclusion, the table below shows the different case ending between the singular and Dual nouns. The plural will be introduced in later lessons.

Case Ending	Singular	Dual	Plural		
			Sound Plural		Broken Plural
			Masculine	Feminine	
Nominative Case **مرفوع**	ــــ ُ ــــ	ـــانِ	ـــونَ	اتٌ	ـ ُ ـ
Accusative Case **منصوب**	ــــ َ ــــ	ـــيْـنِ	ـــيـنَ	اتٍ	ـ َ ـ
Genitive Case **مجرور**	ــــ ِ ــــ	ـــيْـنِ	ـــيـنَ	اتٍ	ـ ِ ـ

Note: We will learn about the plural case ending in future lessons.

Activity 6: Change the underlined words to the dual, pay close attention to the function of the ach word in the sentence:

1. في الحقيبةِ، كراسةٌ و كتابٌ
----
2. البنتُ أكلتْ تفاحةً
----
3. هذه البنتُ جميلةٌ
----
4. هذا الطالبُ مع مدرسِ اللغة العربية
----
5. هذه الحافلةُ كبيرةٌ
----
6. هذه الطالبةُ مع الأستاذةِ
----
7. هذا كتابُ اللغة العربية
----
8. هذه مَدرسةٌ كبيرةٌ
----

9. هذه سيارةٌ جديدةٌ
----
10. هذا بيتٌ قديمٌ
----
11. هذا مِفتاحُ البيتِ
----
12. هذه مُعلمةٌ جديدةٌ
----
13. هذه بنتٌ صغيرةٌ
----
14. هذه شجرةُ برتقال

Activity 7: : Change the underlined nouns/ verbs to the dual form, pay close attention to the function of the each word in the sentence:

1. في هذه الحقيبة كراسةٌ واحدةٌ و كتابٌ واحدٌ
____
2. الولدُ أكل تفاحةً واحدةً
____
3. هذه السيارةُ جديدةٌ و جميلةٌ
____
4. الطالبُ ذهبَ مع المُدرسةِ
____
5. هذه الحافلةُ ستذهب إلى المدرسةِ الثانويَّةِ
____
6. هذه الطالبةُ مع الأستاذةِ
____
7. هذا كتابُ اللغةِ الألمانيَّةِ

____
8. هذا بيتٌ قديمٌ
____
9. هذه المزرعةُ كبيرةٌ و جميلةٌ
____
10. هذه المُعلمةُ جديدةٌ
____

Lesson 10

Number Phrase For The Numbers 1 & 2

- The **nouns** for the numbers **"one" and "two"** aways precede the number.
- The number following the noun is treated as an adjective.
- The number will take the **same ending case** as the noun and **same gender**.

English	In a phrase	Singular word
One book	كِتَابٌ وَاحِدٌ	كِتابٌ
Two chairs	كُرْسِيَّانِ اِثْنَانِ	كُرْسِيٌّ
One Car	سَيَّارة واحِدَة	سَيَّارَةٌ
Two Notebooks	كُراسَتان اِثْنَتانِ	كُرَّاسَةٌ

F	M
وَاحِدَة	وَاحِدٌ
اِثْنَتَانِ	اثْنَانِ
ثَلاثَة	ثَلاثْ
أَرْبَعَة	أَرْبَعْ
خَمْسَة	خَمْس
سِتَّة	سِتٌّ
سَبْعَة	سَبْعْ
ثَمانِيَة	ثَمانْ
تِسْعَة	تِسْعْ
عَشَرَة	عَشَرْ

Examples

- In Arabic the numbers اثنتان/ اِثْنَانِ/ & وَاحِدٌ / واحدة are usually omitted.
- The single or the dual form is considered sufficient to suggest the meaning.
- The words / اثنتانِ/ اِثْنَانِ & وَاحِدٌ / واحدة are used for emphasis

Dual	Singular	Dual	Singular	Dual	Singular
قلمان	قلم	كُوبان	كُوب	سَيَّارَتان	سَيَّارَة
Two pens	**One pen**	**Two cups**	**One cup**	**Two cars**	**One car**

Examples in sentences	
هَذان قلمان	1) هذا قَلَمٌ
هاتان كُرَّاسَتان	2) هذه كُرَّاسة
الدرسانِ في هذيْنِ الكِتابيْنِ	3) الدرسُ في هذا الكِتابِ
المفتاحانِ في هاتيْن السَيَّارتيْن	4) المِفتاح في هَذِه السَيَّارَة

Transform the following sentences into Dual

هذا وَلَدٌ صغير

هذه بِنْتٌ جميلة

هذا الطالب ممتاز

4. هذا رقم كبير

5. هذه حقيبة قديمة

6. هذا معلم جديد

7. هذه مدرسة تونسية

Dual Demonstrative Pronouns For (Nearby) Distances

Feminine			Masculine		
Plural	Dual	Singular	Plural	Dual	Singular
هَـؤلاءِ	هــاتان Nominative	هَــذِه	هَـؤلاء	هـَذان Nominative	هذا
	هاتيْـن (Accusative & genitive)			هـَذيْـن (Accusative & genitive)	

Examples in sentences:	
1. One notebook is in my desk	في مَكْتَبِي كُـرَّاسة وَاحِدةٌ.
2. I have one pen	مَعيِ قَـلَم واحِد
3. One carpet is in the room	فيِ الغُرْفَة، سَجَّادَة وَاحِدَة
4. These are two pens	هَذَانِ قَلَمَانِ اِثْنَان
5. I have two cars	عِنْدِي سَيَّارتَانِ اِثْنَتَانِ

Activity 1: Write the following nouns twice, once with the number <u>ONE</u> and once with the number <u>TWO</u> in <u>Arabic</u>, review the rule before beginning:

Dual	Singular	The word
مُمَرِضَانِ اِثْنَانِ	مُمَرِض واحِد	1. مُمَرِّضٌ
		2. أُذُنٍ
		3. أَرْنَبٌ
		4. تُفَّاحةٍ
		5. طَبِيبٌ
		6. لَيْمُونةٌ
		7. مَرِيضٌ
		8. نَظَّارةٍ
		9. كُرَّاسَةً
		10. عَـيْنٌ

Activity 2: Write the following nouns twice, once with the number ONE and once with the number TWO in Arabic using the appropriate demonstrative pronoun, review the rule before beginning, review your answers with your partner.

Dual	Singular	The word
هَاتَانِ يَدانِ اِثْنَتانِ	هَذِه يَدٌ وَاحِدَةٌ	(1 يَدُ F.
		(2 حَمَّامٍ M.
		(3 زَهْرَةٌ
		(4 حَوْضٍ M.
		(5 ذُبابَةً
		(6 صحفيٌ M.
		(7 بُرْتُقالَةٍ
		(8 ثَوْرٌ
		(9 ثَعْلَبٍ
		(10 جَزِيرَةً

Number Phrase (From 3 to 10)

The following rules apply:	
1) The number always **precedes** the noun	ثَلاثَةُ أولادٍ
2) The **noun** should always be in **plural** form; however, the **number** always appear in **singular** form.	أَرْبَعُ سياراتٍ
3) The **number** of the **Masculine** noun is always Feminine	سَبْعَةُ أقلامٍ
4) The **number** of the **Feminine** noun is always masculine	عَشَرُ كراساتٍ
5) The number will take different cases according to the function of the word in the sentence, but the **noun** will always take the **genitive** case.	خَمْسَةُ أَطفالٍ [1]
6) The noun is mostly indefinite; therefore, "Tanwin with kasrah" may apply.	تِسْعُ بَناتٍ

Child/ Children[1] طفل / أطفال

Singular form of the noun	Examples in sentences:
غُرْفَة	1. في البَيْتِ ثَلاث غُرَفٍ
بَاب	2. في المدرسةِ خَمْسَة أَبْوابٍ
تُفَّاحَة	3. في الطبقِ أَرْبَع تُفَّاحاتٍ
قَلَم	4. في الحقيبةِ أَرْبَعَة أَقْلامٍ

ACTIVITY 3: In full sentences, answer the following questions using the stated number. The possible plural of each noun is listed for you. Include the diacritic mark. Check your answers with your partner.

أقلام// كتب // كراسات // طلاب // بنات // دولارات // أبواب // حافلات// أَطِبَّاءْ // صَناديِق

Notes	Answer	Question
	معي خَمْسَة أَقْلامٍ	1. كَمْ قلماً مَعَكَ؟ 5
		2. كَمْ كتاباً هُناك؟ 8
Bag		3. كم كُرَّاسَةً في الحَقِيبَة؟ 2
		4. كم طالباً في الصَّف ؟ 6
		5. كم بنتاً عِنْدَكِ؟ 3
Pocket		6. كم دولاراً في جَيْبِكَ؟ 1
		7. كم باب في الصف؟ 4
		8. كم حافِلَة في المَدْرَسَة؟ 9
Hospital		9. كم طَبيب في المُسْتَشْفَى؟ 7
Box // storage		10. كم صُنْدوق في المَخْزَن؟ 8

Dual Personal Pronoun

Verb: To Go ذَهَبَ			
Present المضارع	Past الماضي	الضمائر	Personal pronouns
أَذْهَبُ	ذَهَبْتُ	أَنا	I
تَـذْهَبُ	ذَهَبْتَ	أنتَ	You M.
تَذْهَبِـين	ذَهَبْتِ	أنتِ	You F.
يَـذْهَبُ	ذَهَـبَ	هُوَ	He
تَـذْهَبُ	ذَهَبَتْ	هِيَ	She
تَـذْهَبَـــانِ	ذَهَبْـتُمَا	أَنْـتُـما	You Two M.
تَـذْهَبَـــانِ	ذَهَبْـتُمَا	أَنْـتُـما	You Two F.
يَـــذْهَبَـــانِ	ذَهَـبَـــا	هُـــمُـــا	They Two M.(2 he)
تَـــذْهَبَـــانِ	ذَهَـبَـتَـــا	هُـــمُـــا	They Two F(2 she).
نَـذْهَبُ	ذَهَبْنَا	نَحْنُ	We
تَـذْهَبُـونَ	ذَهَبْـتُم	أَنْتُمْ.	You.P. M
تَـذْهَبْنَ	ذَهَبْتُنَّ	أَنْتُنَ	You.P.F.
يَـذْهَبُونَ	ذَهَبُوا	هُمْ	They M.
يَـذْهَبْنَ	ذَهَبْـنَ	هَنَّ	They F.

Conjugate verb _____ فَـعَـلَ ______

المضارع Present	المـاضـي Past	الضمير Pronoun
		أَنـا
		أنْتَ
		أنْـتِ
		هُـوَ
		هِــيَ
		أَنْتُما
		أَنْتُما
		هُما
		هُما

Conjugate verb _____ دَخَلَ ______

المضارع **Present**	المــاضــي **Past**	الضمير **Pronoun**
		أَنــا
		أنْتَ
		أنْــتِ
		هُــوَ
		هِـــيَ
		أَنْتُما
		أَنْتُما
		هُما
		هُما

Conjugate verb _____لَعِـب_____ ______

المضارع **Present**	المــاضــي **Past**	الضمير **Pronoun**
		أَنــا
		أنْتَ
		أنْــتِ
		هُــوَ
		هِــيَ
		أَنْتُما
		أَنْتُما
		هُما
		هُما

Activity 1: Use your previously learned vocabulary to form sentences about your life and your family. Work with your classmate.

.1

.2

.3

.4

.5

.6

.7

.8

.9

.10

Activity 2: Create a dialogue with your classmate, introduce yourselves to each other including your family, work, and education.

	.1
	.2
	.3
	.4
	.5

Verb Conjugation – Singular, Duals, and Plural Pronouns

Verb: To Go ذَهَبَ			
المضارع Present	الماضي Past	الضمائر	Personal pronouns
أَذْهَبُ	ذَهَبْتُ	أَنا	I
تَذْهَبُ	ذَهَبْتَ	أنتَ	You M.
تَذْهَبِينَ	ذَهَبْتِ	أنتِ	You F.
يَذْهَبُ	ذَهَبَ	هُوَ	He
تَذْهَبُ	ذَهَبَتْ	هِيَ	She
تَذْهَبَانِ	ذَهَبْتُمَا	أَنْتُما	You Two M.
تَذْهَبَانِ	ذَهَبْتُمَا	أَنْتُما	You Two F.
يَذْهَبَانِ	ذَهَبَا	هُمُا	They Two M.(2 he)
تَذْهَبَانِ	ذَهَبَتَا	هُمُا	They Two F(2 she).
نَذْهَبُ	ذَهَبْنَا	نَحْنُ	We
تَذْهَبُونَ	ذَهَبْتُم	أَنْتُمْ.	You.P. M
تَذْهَبْنَ	ذَهَبْتُنَّ	أَنْتُنَ	You.P.F.
يَذْهَبُونَ	ذَهَبُوا	هُمْ	They M.
يَذْهَبْنَ	ذَهَبْنَ	هَنَّ	They F.

Conjugate verb _____ ______

المضارع Present	الماضي Past	الضمائر	Personal pronouns
		أَنا	I .1
		أنتَ	You M. .2
		أنتِ	You F. .3
		هُوَ	He .4
		هِيَ	She .5
		أَنْـتُـمـا	You Two M. .6
		أَنْـتُـمـا	You Two F. .7
		هُـــمُـــا	They Two M.(2 he) .8
		هُـــمُـــا	They Two F(2 she). .9
		نَحْنُ	We .10
		أَنْتُمْ.	You.P. M .11
		أَنْتُنَ	You.P.F. .12
		هُمْ	They M. .13
		هَنَّ	They F. .14

Possessive Pronouns

Possessive pronouns indicate the possession of something. In Arabic, these pronouns are suffixed to the noun that's owned.

Meaning	Examples: كِتاب	Possessive Pronoun	Independent Pronoun	
My Book	كِـتابِـي	ي	أَنـَا	I
Your Book	كِـتابُـكَ	كَ	أَنْـتَ	You M.
Your Book	كِـتابُـكِ	كِ	أَنْـتِ	You F.
His Book	كِـتابُـهُ	ـهُ	هُـوَ	He
Her Book	كِـتابُـهَا	هَـا	هِـيَ	She
Our Book	كتابـنَا	نَا	نَحْنُ	We
Your Book – P.	كـتابـكُم	كُم	أَنْتُم	You All
Your Book – P. F.	كـتابـكُنَّ	كُنَّ	أَنْتُنَّ	You All F.
Their Book	كـتابـهُم	هُم	هُم	They
Theor Book – F.	كـتابـهُنَّ	هُنَّ	هُنَّ	They F.
Your Book - Dual	كـتابُـكُـما	كُما	أنتما	You Tow M. & F.
Their Book - Dual	كتابُـهُما	هُما	هما	They Both M. & F.

If the noun that's owned ends in (ـة), It must be untied and made into a ت before attaching the pronoun as a suffix.

Meaning	Examples: كُرَّاسة	Possessive Pronoun	Independent Pronoun	
My Book	كُراسَتِي	ي	أَنـا	I
Your Book	كُراستُكَ	كَ	أَنْـتَ	You M.
Your Book	كُراستُكِ	كِ	أَنْـتِ	You F.
His Book	كُراستُهُ	ـهُ	هُـوَ	He
Her Book	كُراستُـهَـا	هَـا	هِـيَ	She
Our Book	كُراستُـنَـا	نَا	نَحْنُ	We
Your Book – P.	كُراستُـكُم	كُم	أنْتُم	You All
Your Book – P. F.	كُراستُـكُـنَّ	كُنَّ	أنْتُنَّ	You All F.
Their Book	كُراستُـهُم	هُم	هُم	They
Theor Book – F.	كُراستُـهُنَّ	هُنَّ	هُنَّ	They F.
Your Book - Dual	كُراستُكُـما	كُما	أنتما	You Tow M. & F.
Their Book - Dual	كُراستُهُما	هُما	هما	They Both M. & F.

Dialogue 10: Chatting with Two Friends over the weekend

أَيْمَنْ	أَيْنَ سَتَـذْهَـبانِ فِي عُـطْـلَة نِهايَة الأُسْبُوع يا أَمْجَـد و يا عُمر؟
أَمْجَـد	سَنذْهَـبُ إلى السِّـينِما، هَـلْ تَـذْهَبُ مَعَـنـا؟
أيمن	فِي أَيّ يَوْم؟
عُمَر	فِي صباح يَوْم السَّـبْتِ.
أيمن	لا، آسِـف أَنا مَـشْغُول جِداً في صباح يَوْم السَّبْت.
	هل تَـذْهَـبانِ مَعي إِلىَ السِّينِما في يَوْم الأَحَد؟
أَمْجَد	نَعَـم، سَنذْهبُ مَعَـكَ يَوْم الأَحَدْ.
أَيْمَن	مُمْتاز.
عُمَر	هل سَـتَـذْهَبُ مَعَنا في سَـيَّـارتِـنـا ؟
أيمن	نَعَم، نَذْهبُ كَـلُّـنـا في سـيَّـارة واحِدة.
أمجد	مُمْـتـاز، إلى الـلِّـقاءِ في يَـوْمِ الأَحَد صباحاً.

Write Dialogue 10

أَيْمَنْ

أَمْجَـد

أيمن

عُمَر

أيمن

أَمْجَد

أَيْمَن

عُمَر

أيمن

أمجد

Activity3: Translate Dialogue 10. Higlight the dual cases.

أَيْمَنْ

أَمْجَـد

أيمن

عُمَر

أيمن

أَمْجَد

أَيْمَن

عُمَر

أيمن

أمجد

General Practice Activities

Translate the following Sentences

1) أنا أكتب في الكراسة

2) الورقة بيضاء

3) أنا أكلت التفاحة

4) أنا أحب البرتقال

5) أذن أخي كبيرة

6) عندي أمل كبير

7) أنا أحب البطيخ و الفراولة

8) لون الثلج أبيض

9) أبي مهندس

10) أمي طبيبة

11) أختي معلمة

12) أخي ممرض

13) هذا القلم أزرق

14) بيت جدتي أصفر

15) كتاب اللغة العربية برتقالي

16) ألوان جامعة نيفادا، أبيض و أزرق

17) غرفتي وردية

18) الجامعة قريبة من البيت

19) مزرعة جدي كبيرة

20) هذا طالب جديد

21) سيارتي فضية

22) هذه التفاحة حمرا

23) نظّارتي ذهبية

24) حقيبة أبي بنية

25) صاحب أخي ألمانيّ

26) أنا أرسم في الكراسة

27) أنا أحب هذه القصة

28) هذه فراشة بنفسجية ، هي جميلة.

29) في الجامعة مكتبة كبيرة

30) طاولة الأستاذ كبيرة

31) القمر جميل

32) الشمس دافِئة

33) الولد و البنت في الحديقة

34) المقال في الجريدة، اليوم

35) هذه شجرة برتقال

37. هذه نجمة صغيرة

38. شمسيتي حمراء

39. اليوم هو يوم الإثنين

40. أمي بخير و الحمدلله

41. ثوبي أحمر و أسود

42. الطبيب في العيادة

43. چون هو زميلي في صف اللغة العربية

44. أنا أمريكية من ولاية " كولورادو"

45. هذا كتاب مدرسي

46. صديقي "سامر" مصريّ

47. أنا أسكن مع جدتي

48. المدينة الجامعية كبيرة

49. أنا أحب موسيقى " بيتهوفن"

50. أنا أذهب إلى الكلية بسيارتي الوردية

51. بيت جدي قديم و كبير

52. عندي أخت و أخ

53. حافلة الجامعة كبيرة

54. **في الغرفة سجادة صغيرة**

55. **المدينة الجامعية قريبة جداً من الجامعة**

Part Two

LESSON 11

Dialogue 11: Introductions

ماجِد	مَرْحَباً
سَلْمَى	أَهْـلاً و سَـهْلاً
ماجد	اِسْمي ماجِد إِبْراهيم، وَ ما اِسْـمُـكِ؟
سلمى	اِسْمي سَلْمى الـنَّـادي.
ماجد	أَهْـلا بِكِ تَـشَـرَّفْـنا.
سلمى	مِـن أَيْنَ أَنْتَ يا ماجِد؟
ماجد	أَنـا مِـنَ العِراق، مِن مَدينة المُوصِل، وَ أَنْـتِ؟
سلمى	أَنا مِنْ مِصْر، مِنْ مَدِيـنَـةِ القَاهِرَة.

Dialogue 11 Vocabulary list

1.	Where	أَيْنَ	2.	My name	اِسْمي
3.	Iraq	العِراق	4.	From	مِـن
5.	Cairo	القَاهِرَة	6.	Egypt	مِصْر

Activity 1 a: Re-write dialogue 1

Activity 1b: Answer the following questions in Arabic:

1. **What is your name?**
2. **How are you?**
3. **Who are you?**
4. **How is it going ?**
5. **Is it going alright?**

Activity 2 a: Create a similar real-life situation similar to dialogue 1 in the space provided below, then role play with your class partner.:

Dialogue 12: Requesting Information

لُبْنـى	أَهْـلاً مُـنى
منى	أَهْـلاً لُبْنـَى
لبنى	مَاذا تَـفْعَلِـيـنَ هُـنا؟
منى	أنـا أَعْـمَـلُ هُـنـا وَ هَذا مَكْـتَـبـي.
لبنى	وَ أَيْـنَ مَـكْـتَـبُ المُدير؟
منى	مَـكْـتـبُ المُدير هُناك بِـالقُرْبِ مِنَ البَاب الرَّئيسِـيِّ.
لبنى	شُـكْراً يا مُنى.
منى	عَـفْـواً.

Dialogue 12 Vocabulary

1.	Verb To do	تَفْعَلِـينَ / أَعْـمَـلُ	2.	What	مَاذا
3.	The manager	المُدير	4.	My office	مَكْـتَـبي
5.	The door	البَاب	6.	Near by	بِالقُرْبِ
			7.	The main	الـرَّئيسـيّ

Activity 2 b: Write dialogue 2

Activity 3: Create a similar real-life situation similar to dialogue 2 in the space provided below, then Create a dialogue with your class partner about a situation in real life. Use all the previous vocabulary you learned:

Dialogue 13: Introduce Your Friends To Each Other

خالد	صباحُ الخَيْر يا حُسام
حُسام	صباحُ الخيْر يا خالد، هَذِهِ صَديقَتي أَسْماء.
	أسماء، هَذا صَديقِي خالِد.
خالد	أهلاً يا أسْماء، تَشَرَّفنا.
أسْماء	أهْلاً يا خالِد، مَرْحباً بِكَ.
خالد	هَلْ أنْتِ طالِبَة مَعَنا هُنا فِي الجامِعَة؟
أسْماء	نَعَم، أنا طالِبَة في كُلِّيَّة العُلوم السِّياسِيَّة، وَ ماذا عَنْكَ؟
خالد	أنا طالِبٌ في كُلية التِّجارَة مَعَ حُسام.
	وَ أحياناً، أعْمَلُ في مَطْعَمِ الجَامِعَة في المَساء.
أسماء	فُرْصَة سَعِيدَة يا خالِد.
حسام	هَلْ تَعْمَلُ هَذا المَساء يا خالِد؟
خالد	نعم، أعْملُ في المساء بَعْدَ المُحاضَرَة الأَخِيرَة.
حسام	إذَن، إلَى اللِّقاء غَداً في الصَّباح.

Communicative Activity : In Group of three, introduce one classmate to another.

Activity 4 a: Re-write dialogue 13

Dialogue 13 Vocabulary			
1. College	كلية	2. My F. Friend	صديقتي
3. Sciences	العلوم	4. With us	معنا
5. Politics	السياسية	6. About you	عنكَ
7. With	مع	8. Commerce	التجارة
9. Restaurant	مطعم	10. I work	أعمل
11. Opportunity	فرصة	12. The evening	المساء
13. Does it/Is it	هل	14. Happy	سعيدة
15. After	بعد	16. Yes	نعم
17. The last	الأَخِيرة	18. Lecture	المُحاضَرة
19. Until meeting	إلـى اللِّقاء	20. Then	إذن
21. The morning	الصَّباح	22. Tomorrow	غداً
23.		24. Sometimes	أحياناً

Activity 4 b: Answer the following questions in Arabic:

1. Are you a student?

---

2. What do you study?

---

3. Do you work?

---

4. Where do you work?

---

5. When do you go to work ?

Activity 4 c: Pretend that you are one of the 3 peoples in dialogue 3, create a dialogue with a similar situation in the space provided below, then role play with your classmates:

Dialogue 14: Do You Like ?

چون يا مارْك، هَلْ تُحِبُ مَدِينَة "سان فرانْسيسكو"؟

مارك لا، أنا لا أُحِبُ هَذِهِ المَدينَة وَ لَكِنْ أُحِبُ مَدينَة " سان دييجو" في جَنوب وِلايَة كاليفورنيا.

چون و أَنْتَ يا چيمْس، هَل تُحِبُ مَدينَة "سان فرانسيسكو"؟

چيمس نَعم، أنا أُحِبُ مَدينَة " سان فرانسيسكو" جِداً، هِيَ مَدينَةٌ جَميلَةٌ جِداً.

چون هَلْ ذَهَبْتَ إلى المَدينَةِ الصِّينيَّةِ هُناك؟

چيمس نَعم نَعَم، ذَهَبتُ إلى هُناك مَعَ أُسْرَتي عِدَّةُ مَرَّاتٍ.

Communicative Activity : In pairs, role play the dialogue with your class partner, personalized it to your experience.

Dialogue 14 Vocabulary			
1. **No / Not**	لا	2. You love	تُحِبُ
3. **South**	جَنـوب	4. But	لَكِنْ
5. **You went**	ذَهَبْتَ	6. Beautiful	جَميلَة
7. **Several**	عِدَّة	8. Chinese	الصِّيـنيَّـة
		9. Times	مرَّة / مَـرَّات

Activity 14 c: Write Dialogue 4

Activity 4 d: Answer the following questions in Arabic:

1. **Do you like the city of New York?**

---

2. **Do you like the Carson City?**

---

3. **What city do you like the most on the East coast?**

---

4. **Why do you like this city?**

---

5. **Did you go to a specific landmark at this city?**

---

6. **How many times did you visit this landmark?**

Activity 5: Create a similar real-life situation similar to dialogue 4 in the space provided below, then role play with your class partner.

Dialogue 15: Saying Good Bye

چون   يا چيمس، هَلْ أَنْتَ جاهِزٌ لِلسَّفَر، غداً؟

چيمس   نَعَم، أنا جاهِزٌ وَ شُكراً عَلى كُلِّ شَيءٍ.

چون   عَفْواً يا چيمس، مَتَى تَذْهَبُ إلى المَطار؟

چيمس   غداً صباحاً، إنْ شاءَ اللَّه.

چون   إذَنْ، إلى اللِّقاء في الكُوَيْت إنْ شَاءَ اللَّه.

چيمس   مَعَ السَّلامَة وَ إلى اللِّقاء.

Communicative Activity : In pairs, role play the dialogue with your class partner, personalized it to your experience.

Activity 6: Write Dialogue 15

Dialogue 15: Vocabulary			
1. The airport	المَطار	2. Ready	جـاهِـزٌ
3. The meeting	اللِّقـاء	4. For travel	لِـلـسَفَر (ل+ السفر)
5. Safety	السَّلامَة	6. Tomorrow	غَداً
7. Thing	شَيءٍ	8. Every	كُـلِّ
9. Then	إِذَنْ	10. When?	مَـتـى

Activity 7: Answer the following question in Arabic:

How do you say "Until tomorrow" in Arabic?

How do you say "Be safe" in Arabic?

How do you say "Thank you for everything" in Arabic?

How do you say 'I am ready" in Arabic?

Word Order - Pronouns

In Arabic, the first-person pronoun comes first in the sentence: أنا و أنتَ /I and you.

It is the reverse of the usual English order: you and I

When there is a series of pronouns, or pronouns and nouns, the regular order in Arabic is: first person, second person, third person, noun.

Examples	
1. **I & Medhad**	أنا وَ مِدْحَت.
2. **You & Hoda**	أنتَ وَ هُدَى.
3. **You & your sister**	أنْتِ و أُخْتُكِ.
4. **I & my Family**	أنا وَ أُسْرَتي.
5. **I & My Brother & my sister**	أنا و أَخي و أُخْتي

Arabic Calligraphy

Arabic calligraphy is the artistic practice of handwriting and calligraphy based on the Arabic alphabet. It is known in Arabic as khatt (Arabic: خط), derived from the word 'line', 'design', or 'construction'. Kufic is the oldest form of the Arabic script.

Although most Islamic calligraphy is in Arabic and most Arabic calligraphy is Islamic, the two are not identical. Coptic Christian manuscripts in Arabic, for example, may make use of calligraphy. Likewise, there is Islamic calligraphy in Persian.

Classroom Communication

الأُسْـتاذ/ة: مَا مَعْـنى " سَـيَّارَة"؟

What is the meaning of سيارة?

الطَّالِب: يا أُسْتاذ/ة، أنا *أَعْـرِفُ الجَـواب

Professor, I know the anwer

الطالِب: يا أُسْتاذ/ة: عِنْدي سُؤَال

Professor, I have a question

الأُسْتاذ/ة: تَـفَضَّل، ما هُوَ السُّؤال؟

Professor: What is the question?

*I know

My Family House

بَيْتُ أُسْرَتِـي

أَسْكنُ في بَيْتٍ كَبيرٍ وَ جَديدٍ مَعَ عَائِلَتي.

هَذِهِ صُورَة أُسْرَتي وَ هَذِهِ أُخْتي الكَبيرَة وَ هَذَا أَخي الصَّغِير.

هَذا أَثــاثٌ جَديدٌ وَ حَديثٌ.

هُناك في المَطْبَخ، مَوْقِد وَ غَسَّالَة صُحون وَ مَايْكْرووِيف.

و أَيْـضـاً غَـسَّـالـة و نَـشَّـافَـة.

وَ مَـاكِـينَة قَـهْوَة

وَ تِـلْـفازٌ كَـبـيرٌ وَ حَـدِيثٌ

وَ تِليفوناتٍ مَحْمُولَة قَدِيمَة

وَ تِـلِيفَونٌ أَرْضِيٌّ

وَ دَرَّاجَة رِيـاضِيَّة

أَقْـضِـي عُـطْـلَـةَ عِيدُ المِيلادِ مَعَ أُسْـرَتي في بَـيْـتِـنا الكَبِير.

Vocabulary List

1. **Dryer**	نَشَّافَة	2. Fridge	ثَلاَّجَة
3. **Coffee machine**	ماكينَة قَهْوة	4. Washer	غَسَّالة
5. **Fan**	مَرْوَحة	6. Stove	مَوْقِد
7. **Freezer**	فِريزَر	8. Cell phone	مَحْمول/ جَوَّال
9. **Television**	تِلْفاز / تِلْفِزيون	10. Phone	هاتِف/ تِليفون
11. **Microwave**	مايْكْرُووِيف	12. Vacuum cleaner	مَكْنَسَة
13. **Bike**	درَّاجة	14. Air conditioning	تَكْييف/ مُكَيِّف / مبرِّد
15. **Grill**	شَوَّايَة	16. Heater	مِدْفَئَة

Activity 8: Talk with your partner about similar appliances you have or wish to have, such as "What is in your barracks room?" or at your parents or friends' houses. Try to use some adjectives like small, big, old, and new. These phrases will help you get started.

في البَيْت	في المَكْتَب	في غُرْفة المَدينَة الجامِعِيَة

Activity 9 a: Fill in the blank using the vocabulary you have learned.

أنا من .... لوس أنجلوس في .... كاليفورنيا. أدرس

.... في .... كاليفورنيا.

أبي........... و أمي .... و

أخي........... و أختي ....

عندي .... و أخت و أيضاً عندي

.... هوندا حمراء. أسكن في

.... الجامعية مع ....

چون.

بيت .... كبير و جميل. في البيت

.... جديد و حديث.

هناك في مطبخ البيت ....

و ....و ....

Activity 9 b: Answer the following questions in Arabic:

1. Where do you live?

---

2. Describe you're your family house?

---

3. Do you have a picture with your family?

---

4. Describe the furniture in your house?

---

5. What appliances do you have in the kitchen?

---

6. How many cell phones do you have?

---

7. Do you have a bike?

---

8. Where do you spend the Christmas holiday?

Classroom Communication

چون: يا أُسْتاذ/ة عِنْدي سؤال، كَيْفَ أَقول Classmate بالعَـربيَّة؟

Professor, I have a question, How to say classmate in Arabic?

الأُسْـتاذ/ة: زمِيل /ة

چون: يا أستاذ/ة ، كيف أكتب هذه الكلمة؟

Professor, How to write this word?

الأستاذ: ز م ي ل = زمــيـــل

چون: يا أُستاذ/ة، ما معْـنى كلِمة "صديق"؟

Professor, What is the meaning of the word "صديق" ?

الأستاذ/ة : Friend

چون: شُكْراً يا أستاذ/ة

Activity 10: Listen to the following words. Identify the short vowel associated with the first letter of each word, then mark it on top of the letter.

1. طماطِم	2. مطيع	3. جبَّار	4. صديق
5. ضفْدع	6. إسْعاف	7. ضريبة	8. صنْدوق
9. جدَّتي	10. كلِيَّة	11. جامِعَة	12. تلْميذ
13. مصيبة	14. تمْرين	15. تـفّاح	16. حافِلة
17. باب	18. قـميص	19. حاسوب	20. مشْكِلة
21. حديقَة	22. بـسْتان	23. شمْس	24. هاتِف
25. حار	26. نخْلة	27. مـنْشار	28. عـلَم

Activity 11: Listen to 15 words pronounced twice. Each word contains on or more of the following letters. ح – ص - هـ - ع - خ – ز - ذ

For each word mark the letter that you recognize then check your answers with your classmates.

ذ	ع	ز	هـ	خ	ع	ص	ح	
								1.
								2.
								3.
								4.
								5.
								6.
								7.
								8.
								9.
								10.
								11.
								12.
								13.
								14.
								15.

Activity 12: Translate the following sentences

1. هذا أَبي وهو أمْريكيٌّ

2. أنا أذْهَبُ إِلىَ الجامِعة بِالحافِـلة العامَّة

3. أُسْتاذَة اللُّغَة العَـربِيَّة، مِنْ مِصْر.

4. أنا أُحِبُّ كُـرَة السَّلَّة.

5. في الغُـرْفَة، طاوِلَة كَبيرَة.

6. هذا الصَّباح، المَقالُ فِي الجَـريدَة.

7. الطَّبيـبُ في المُـسْتَـشْفَى.

8. أنا أَلْعَـبُ كُـرَة السَّلة يَـوْمَ السَّبْت.

9. أنا أدرسُ اللُّغة العَـرَبـيَّة

10. أنا أَسْـكُـنُ في المَدينَة الجامِعيَّة

11. أنا أَسْـكُـنُ فِي مَدينَة "رينو"

12. هَذِهِ أُمِّي الحَـبيبَة.

Activity 13: Translate the following sentences:

1. هل تذْهبُ مَعي إلَى السِّـيـنِـما يَـوْمَ الأَحَد؟

2. هَـذا أُسْـتاذٌ مـُمْتازٌ

3. هـذا القَلَمُ أَحْمَر

4. عِـنْـدي أَخٌ واحِـدٌ

5. المُـدَرِّسانِ فـي المَكْتَبِ الكَـبير.

6. عِـنْدي خَـمْـسةُ أَطْفالٍ.

7. أنا أُحب ُجَدَّتي جِداً

8. سلمى هِيَ أُخْتي الكَبيرَة

9. أنا مَشْغولٌ جِداً يَوْم الأَحَد.

10. مَعي سِتَّة أقْلام في الحَقيبَة

11. نافِذَة الصَّفِ كَبيرَة.

12. كَمْ سَيَّارَة فِضْيَّة هُناك؟

Equational Sentences

Arabic sentences are of two types, those with verbs, called verbal sentences, and those not containing verbs, called equational sentences. Verbal sentences will be introduced in later lesson

The equational sentence consists of two parts, a subject and a predicate

As in English, the subject may be any kind of noun or pronoun, while the predicate may be either of these, as well as adjectives, adverbs, or prepositional phrases.

Arabic equational sentences generally correspond to English sentences in which the verb is "am" is or are that is , a present tense form of verb " to be" .

Examples	
I am John	.1 أَنــا چُون
John is from America	.2 چُـون مِن أمْريكا
This is John	.3 هَذا چُون
John is American	.4 چُـون أمْـرِيكِيٌّ

Interrogatives

If an Arabic sentence contains an interrogative word, that word must come ***first*** in the question sentence:

Examples	
1. who are you?	– مَنْ أَنْتَ؟ – أنا چـون
2. Do you have a pen?	– هَـلْ مَعـكَ قَـلَمٌ؟ – نَعَـم، مَعي قَـلَمٌ
3. How are you?	– كَيْـفَ حَالُـكَ؟ – أنـا بِخَيْـر
4. What is the car's color?	– ما لَـوْنُ السَّبورَةَ؟ – لوْن السَّبورَة أبْيَض
5. What is this John?	– ما هذا يا چـون؟ – هذا كِتابٌ
6. What is this John?	– ما هذِهِ يا چون؟ – هذِهِ طاوِلَةُ الصَّفِ

Activity 14: With your class partner, create a series of short questions and their answers. Write the English equivalent in the opposite column:

------------------------------ ------------------------------	------------------------------ ------------------------------
------------------------------ ------------------------------	------------------------------ ------------------------------
------------------------------ ------------------------------	------------------------------ ------------------------------
------------------------------ ------------------------------	------------------------------ ------------------------------
------------------------------ ------------------------------	------------------------------ ------------------------------
------------------------------ ------------------------------	------------------------------ ------------------------------

Lesson 11 Vocabulary List			
1. **Where**	أَيْنَ	37) My name	إِسْمي
2. **Iraq**	العِراق	38) From	مِـن
3. **Cairo**	القَاهِرَة	39) Egypt	مِصْر
4. **Verb To do**	تَفْعَلِيـنَ / أَعْـمَـلُ	40) What	مَاذا
5. **The manager**	المُديـر	41) My office	مَكْـتَـبي
6. **The door**	البَاب	42) Near by	بِـالقُرْبِ
7. **College**	كلية	43) The main	الـــرَّئِيسِـيّ
8. **Sciences**	العلوم	44) My F. Friend	صديقتي
9. **Politics**	السياسية	45) With us	معنا
10. **With**	مع	46) About you	عنكَ
11. **Restaurant**	مطعم	47) Commerce	التجارة
12. **Opportunity**	فرصة	48) I work	أعمل
13. **Does it/Is it**	هل	49) The evening	المساء
14. **After**	بعد	50) Happy	سعيدة
15. **The last**	الأَخِيرة	51) Yes	نعم
16. **Until meeting**	إِلـى اللِّقاء	52) Lecture	المُحاضَرة

17. **The morning**	الصَّباح	53) Then	إذن
18. **No / Not**	لا	54) Tomorrow	غداً
19. **South**	جَـنـوب	55) Sometimes	أحياناً
20. **You went**	ذَهَبْتَ	56) You love	تُـحِـبُ
21. **Several**	عِدَّة	57) But	لَكِنْ
22. **The airport**	المَطار	58) Beautiful	جَـميلَـة
23. **The meeting**	اللِّقـاء	59) Chinese	الصِّـينـيَّـة
24. **Safety**	السَّلامَة	60) Times	مرَّة / مَـرَّات
25. **Thing**	شَيءٍ	61) Ready	جـاهِـزٌ
26. **Then**	إذَنْ	62) For travel	لِـلـسَـفَـر --- (ل+ السفر)
27. **Dryer**	نَشَّافَة	63) Tomorrow	غداً
28. **Coffee machine**	ماكينَة قَهْوة	64) Every	كُـلِّ
29. **Fan**	مَرْوَحة	65) When?	مَـتـى
30. **Freezer**	فِريزَر	66) Fridge	ثَلاَّجَة
31. **Television**	تِلْفاز / تِلِفِزيون	67) Washer	غَسَّالة
32. **Microwave**	مايْكرُووِيف	68) Stove	مَوْقِد
33. **Bike**	درَّاجة	69) Cell phone	مَحْمول/ جَوَّال

34. **Grill**	شَوَّايَة	70) Phone	هاتِف/ تِليفون
35. **Air conditioning**	تَكْييف/ مُكَيِّف / مبَرِّد	71) Vacuum cleaner	مَكْنَسَة
36. **Heater**	مِدْفَئَة		

LESSON 12

Numbers الأَرْقام

F.	M.
صِفْر	صِفْر
وَاحِدَة	وَاحِدٌ
اِثْنَتَانِ	اِثْنَانِ
ثَلاثَة	ثَلاثْ
أَرْبَعَة	أَرْبَعْ
خَمْسَة	خَمْسْ
سِتَّة	سِتّْ
سَبْعَة	سَبْعْ
ثَمَانِيَة	ثَمَانْ
تِـسْعَة	تِسْعْ
عَـشَرَة	عَـشَرْ

Revisiting Number Phrases For: 1 & 2

I have ONE book	عندي كِتَابْ وَاحِدْ
I have ONE car	عندي سيارة واحدة
I have TWO books	عندي كتابان اثْنَانِ
I have TWO cars	عندي سيارتان اثنتان

The Following Rules Apply

- **The nouns for the numbers "one" and "two" always precede the number.**
- **The number following the noun is treated as an adjective.**
- **The number will take the same ending case as the noun and same gender.**

Note: In Arabic the numbers & واحدة / وَاحِدٌ /اِثْنَانِ /اثنتانِ are usually omitted.

The single or the dual form is considered sufficient to suggest the meaning.

The words اِثْنَانِ /اثنتانِ / & واحدة / وَاحِدٌ are used for emphasis

Let Us Revise The Dual		
Dual Accusitave / Genitive	Dual Nominative	Singular
قلمَيْن	قَـلَمَـانْ	قَلَمْ
سيارتَـيْـنِ	سَيَّارَتـــان	سَيَّارَة

Examples in sentences	
One pen is on my desk	على مَكْـتَبِي، قلمٌ وَاحِدةٌ.
I have one book	مَعَـــــي كِتابٌ واحِدٌ
One window is in the room	فِي الغُرْفَة، نافِذةٌ وَاحِدَةٌ
These are two books	هَذَانِ كتابانِ اِثْـنَـانِ
I have two big libarries	عِنْدِي مَكْـتَبَتَانِ اِثْنَتَانِ كَبيرَتَـانِ
There are two managers in this office	هُـناك مُديرانِ اِثْـنانِ في هذا المَـكْـتبِ.

Number Phrase For Numbers: 3,4,5,6,7,8,9,10

The following rules apply

1. *The number always **precedes** the noun*	ثَلاثَةُ أَقْلامٍ
2. *The **noun** should always be in **plural** form; however, the **number** always appear in **singular** form.*	أَرْبَعُ سَيَّاراتٍ
3. *The **number** of the **Masculine** noun is always <u>Feminine</u>*	سَبْعَةُ أَقْلامٍ
4. *The **number** of the **Feminine** noun is always <u>masculine</u>*	عَشَرُ كُرَّاساتٍ
5. *The number will take different cases according to the function of the word in the sentence, but the **noun** will always take the **genitive** case.*	خَمْسَةُ كُتُبٍ
6. *The noun is mostly indefinite; therefore, "**Tanwin** with kasrah" may apply.*	تِسْعُ بَناتٍ

Examples in sentences	
غُرْفَة	1. في البَيْتِ، ثَلاثُ غُـرَفٍ
بَاب	2. في المَدْرَسَةِ، خَـمْـسَـةُ أَبْـوابٍ
تُـفَّاحَة	3. في الطَّـبَـقِ، أَرْبَعُ تُـفَّـاحاتٍ
كُـرْسيّ	4. في الصَّفِ، سِـتَّةُ كَـراسٍ
قَـلَم	5. في الحـقـيـبـةِ، أَرْبَعَةُ أَقْلامٍ

Activity 1: Write the following nouns 3 TIMES, once with the number ONE quantity, once with the number TWO quantity and once with the given number in the third column, review the rules before beginning, the first one is done for you:

3-10	Dual	Singular	The word
5// خمس ممرضون	هاذان مُمَرِّضَانِ اِثْنَانِ	هذا مُمَرِض واحِد	.1 مُمَرِّضٌ .m
4//			.2 أُذنٍ .f
6//			.3 أَرْنَبٌ .m
7//			.4 تُفَّاحَةً .f
9//			.5 طبيبٌ .m
10//			.6 ليمونةٌ .f
9//			.7 مريضٌ.m
6//			.8 نظَّارةً.f
5//			.9 كُراسَةٍ .f
6//			.10 عَيْنٌ .f
Plurals: مُمرِّضون، آذان، أرانِب، تُفَّاحات، أطِبَّاء، ليْمونات، مَرْضى، نظَّارات، كُراسات، عُيون			

Activity 2: Write the following nouns 3 times, once with the number ONE quantity, once with the number TWO quantity and once with the given number in the third column, review the rules before beginning, the first one is done for you; pay close attention to the ending case of each word. When you are done review your answers with you're a classmate partner.

3-10	Form the sentence in Dual form	Form the sentence in Singular form	The word
10// عشرُ سيارات	هَاتَانِ يَدانِ اِثْنَتانِ	هَذِهِ يَـدٌ وَاحِدَةٌ	1. سيارة
3//			2. قلم
5//			3. باب
7//			4. مكتب
6//			5. مكتبة
5//			6. مهندس
7//			7. طاولة
8//			8. دجاجة
9//			9. شجرة
10//			10. أستاذ
سيارات ، أقلام ، أبواب، مكاتب، مكتبات، مهندسون، طاولات، دجاجات، شجرات، أساتذة			

Numbers 11 To 19

Feminine	Masculine	Number
إِحْدَى عَشْرَةَ	أَحَـدَ عَشَرَ	١١
اثْـنَـتَا عَشْرَةَ	اِثْـنَـا عَشَرَ	١٢ Nominative
اثْنَتَـيْ عَشْرَةَ	اِثْـنَـي عَشَر مُهَنْدِسًا	١٢ Genitive Accusative
ثَلاثَ عَشْرَةَ	ثلاثَةَ عَشَرَ	١٣
أَرْبَعَ عَشْرَةَ	أَرْبَعَةَ عَشَرَ	١٤
خَمْسَ عَشْرَةَ	خَمْسَةَ عَشَرَ	١٥
سِتَّ عَشْرَةَ	سِتَّةَ عَشَرَ	١٦
سَبْعَ عَشْرَةَ	سَبْعَةَ عَشَرَ	١٧
ثَمَانِيَ عَشْرَةَ	ثَمَانِيَةَ عَشَرَ	١٨
تِسْعَ عَشْرَةَ	تِسْعَةَ عَشَرَ	١٩

Number Phrase for Numbers: 11 - 19

Numbers 11 & 12

Feminine	Masculine	Number
إِحْدَى عَشْرَةَ أُسْتاذةً	أَحَـدَ عَشَرَ أُسْتاذاً	١١
(اثنتان) اثْنَتا عَشْرَةَ مُهَنْدِسَةً	(اثنان) اِثْـنـا عَشَرَ مُهَنْدِساً	١٢ Nominative
(اثنتيْنِ) اثْنَتَي عَشْرَةَ مُهَنْدِسَةً	(اثنينِ) اِثْنَي عَشَر مُهَنْدِسًا	١٢ Genitive Accusative

The Following Rules Apply

The number precedes the noun

The number agrees with the nouns in gender

In the accusative & genitive case, the ending case of 2 in number 12 must be just ي while dropping the ن is of the dual (ين)

In the nominative case, the ending case of 2 in number 12 must be just ا while dropping the ن of the dual (ان)

Number Phrase for 13-19

ثلاث عَشْرَةَ مُدَرِّسَةَ	ثلاثةَ عَشَرَ طالباً	١٣
أرْبَعَ عَشْرَةَ قِصَّةً	أرْبَعَةَ عَشَرَ كِتَابًا	١٤
خَمْسَ عَشْرَةَ سَاعَةً	خَمْسَةَ عَشَرَ يَوْماً	١٥
سِتَّ عَشْرَةَ دَجَاجَةً	سِتَّةَ عَشَرَ دِيكًا	١٦
سَبْعَ عَشْرَةَ سيارةً	سَبْعَةَ عَشَرَ قلماً	١٧
ثَمَانِي عَشْرَةَ صَدِيقَةً	ثَمَانِيَةَ عَشَرَ صَدِيقـاً	١٨
تِسْعَ عَشْرَةَ سَنَةً	تِسْعَةَ عَشَرَ يَوْماً	١٩

The Following Rules Apply

The first part of these compound number must be in the opposite gender of the noun.
However the second part of the number (عشر/ة) must agree in gender with the noun.
The two parts of the number have a fixed vowel, Fatħa, as ending case.
The noun is in Singular format.

Activity 4: Listen to a series of numbers and write the English equivalent in the space provided.

6)	5)	4)	3)	2)	1)
12)	11)	10)	9)	8)	7)
18)	17)	16)	15)	14)	13)
24)	23)	22)	21)	20)	19)
30)	29)	28)	27)	26)	25)

Activity 5: Listen to a series of numbers and write the English equivalent in the space provided.

6)	5)	4)	3)	2)	1)
12)	11)	10)	9)	8)	7)
18)	17)	16)	15)	14)	13)
24)	23)	22)	21)	20)	19)
30)	29)	28)	27)	26)	25)

Activity 6: : In full sentences, answer the following questions using the number shown with each question. The possible plural of each noun is listed below. Check your answers with your partner.

أقلام// كتب // كراسات // طلاب // بنات // دولارات // أبواب // حافلات// أَطِبَّاءْ // صَناديق

Answer	Question
معي أحدَ عشر قلماً	1) كَمْ قلماً مَعَكَ؟ 11
	2) كَمْ كتاباً هُناكْ؟ 19
	3) كم كُرَّاسَةً في الحَقِـيبَة؟ 12
	4) كم طالباً في الصَّفِ؟ 13
	5) كم بِنْتاً عِنْدَكِ؟ 5
	6) كم دولاراً في جَيْبِكَ؟ 3
	7) كم باباً في الصَّـفِ؟ 9
	8) كم حافِلَةً في المَدْرَسَةْ؟ 18
	9) كم طَبيباً في المُسْتَشْفَى؟ 17
	10) كم صُنْدوقاً في المَخْزَنْ؟ 10

Counting By Tens		
(Accusative Or Genitive Case)	(Nominative Case)	
عِشْرين	عِشْرون	٢٠
ثَلاثين	ثَلاثون	٣٠
أرْبَعين	أرْبَعون	٤٠
خَمْسين	خَمْسون	٥٠
سِتِّين	سِتُّون	٦٠
سَبْعين	سَبْعون	٧٠
ثمانِين	ثَمانون	٨٠
تِسْعين	تِسْعون	٩٠

The following rules apply

The ending case of these numbers must change according to their function in the sentence.

The ending ون changes to ين in the cases of accusative or genitive.

They don't change gender in regard of the noun that follows.

The noun that follows these numbers bust be singular & in the accusative case.

Examples	
(Nominative)	في هذا الكتاب، سَبْعون قصة
(Genitive)	هؤلاء الطلاب في العشرينَ مِن عُمرهم
(Accusative)	أنا أكلتُ عشرينَ تـُفاحةً

Activity 7: Listen to a series of numbers and write the English equivalent in the space provided.

5.	4.	3.	2.	1.
10.	9.	8.	7.	6.
15.	14.	13.	12.	11.
20.	19.	18.	17.	16.

Activity 8: Listen to a series of numbers and write the English equivalent in the space provided.

5.	4.	3.	2.	1.
10.	9.	8.	7.	6.
15.	14.	13.	12.	11.
20.	19.	18.	17.	16.

Counting From 21- 29, 31 -39, etc..

The conjunction و must be used to connect the two digits.

	Feminine	Masculine
Nominative	واحدةٌ و عِشْرونَ قصةً	واحدٌ وعِشْرونَ كتاباً
	اِثنتانِ و ثــلاثــونَ قصةً	اِثنانِ و ثــلاثونَ كتاباً
--------------------	واحدةً و عِشْرينَ قصةً Accusative	واحدٍ وعِشْرينَ كتاباً Genitive
Genitive & Accusative	اِثنتيــْنِ و ثــلاثيــنَ قصةً	اِثنيْنِ و ثــلاثيــنَ كتاباً

Activity 9: Listen to a series of numbers and write the English equivalent in the space provided.

5.	4.	3.	2.	1.
10.	9.	8.	7.	6.
15.	14.	13.	12.	11.
20.	19.	18.	17.	16.

Activity 10: Listen to a series of numbers and write the English equivalent in the space provided.

5.	4.	3.	2.	1.
10.	9.	8.	7.	6.
15.	14.	13.	12.	11.
20.	19.	18.	17.	16.

Activity 11: Listen to a series of numbers and write the English equivalent in the space provided.

5.	4.	3.	2.	1.
10.	9.	8.	7.	6.
15.	14.	13.	12.	11.
20.	19.	18.	17.	16.

Activity 12 : In full sentences, answer the following questions using the number shown with each question. The possible plural of each noun is listed below. Check your answers with your partner.

أقلام// كتب // كراسات // طلاب // بنات // دولارات // أبواب // حافلات// أَطِبَّاءْ // صَناديقْ

Answer	Question
عندي أربعة و ثلاثون قلماً	11) كَمْ قلماً عِنْدَك؟ 34
	12) كَمْ كتاباً هُناكْ؟ 22
	13) كم كُرَّاسَةً في الحَقِـيبَة؟ 23
	14) كم طالباً في الصَّفِ؟ 55
	15) كم بِنْتاً عِنْدَكِ؟ 1
	16) كم دولاراً في جَيْبِكَ؟ 89
	17) كم باباً في الصَّـفِ؟ 3
	18) كم حافِلَةً في المَدْرَسَةْ؟ 12
	19) كم طَبيباً في المُسْتَشْفى؟ 78
	20) كم صُنْدوقاً في المَخْزَنْ؟ 99

The Numbers 100,200,300, etc.				
مِئة / مائة	مِئَتـــان / مِـئَـتـيْـنِ	ثَـلاثُـمِـئَـة	أَرْبَـعُـمِـئَـة	خَـمْـسُـمِـئَـة
سِـتـُّـمِـئَـة	سَـبْـعُـمِـئَـة	ثَمانُمائَة	تِـسْـعُـمِـئَـة	
Hundred/s مِئَة – مِئات				

The Numbers 1000,2000,3000, etc.				
ألف	أَلْـفـانِ / أَلْـفَـيْـنِ	ثَلاثَةُ آلافٍ	أَرْبَعَةَ آلافٍ	خَمْسَةِ آلافٍ
سِتـّـةُ آلافٍ	سَبْعَةُ آلافٍ	ثَمانِيَةُ آلافٍ	تِسْعَةُ آلافٍ	عشرةِ آلافٍ
ألف is a masculine word		Thousand/s أَلْف – آلاَف		

The Numbers 1000000,2000000,etc.				
مِلْيون	مليونانِ / مليونينِ	ثَلاثَةُ ملايين	أَرْبَعَةُ ملايين	خَمْسَةُ ملايين
سِتَّةُ ملايين	سَبْعَةُ ملايين	ثَمانِيَةُ ملايين	تِسْعَةُ ملايين	عشرةُ ملايين
مليون is a masculine word		Million/s مِلْيون - مَلايِـــيـــن		

The Following Rules Apply
The nouns that follow the numbers of hundreds, thousands & millions are always singular & genitive (ending with kasrah in singular case).
There is no gender change needed for these numbers.
The noun is always in a singular form.

Examples

In the library, a million book.	في المكتبةِ، مليونُ كِتـابٍ
In the storage, a million notebook	في المخزنِ، مليونُ كُراسـةٍ
In my library, a thousand book.	في مكتبتي، ألفُ كـتـابٍ
In the book, a thousand story.	في الكتابِ، ألفُ قـصـةٍ
On the table, a hundred plate and a hundred spoon.	على المائدَةِ، مِئةُ طـبـقٍ و مـئـةُ مِلْعَقَةٍ

Activity 13: Listen to a series of numbers and write the English equivalent in the space provided.

5.	4.	3.	2.	1.
10.	9.	8.	7.	6.
15.	14.	13.	12.	11.
20.	19.	18.	17.	16.

Activity 14: Listen to a series of numbers and write the English equivalent in the space provided.

5.	4.	3.	2.	1.
10.	9.	8.	7.	6.
15.	14.	13.	12.	11.
20.	19.	18.	17.	16.

Activity 15: Listen to a series of numbers and write the English equivalent in the space provided.

5.	4.	3.	2.	1.
10.	9.	8.	7.	6.
15.	14.	13.	12.	11.
20.	19.	18.	17.	16.

Activity 16: Listen to a series of numbers and write the English equivalent in the space provided.

5.	4.	3.	2.	1.
10.	9.	8.	7.	6.
15.	14.	13.	12.	11.
20.	19.	18.	17.	16.

Activity 17 : In full sentences, answer the following questions using the number shown with each question. The possible plural of each noun is listed below. Check your answers with your partner.

أقلام// كتب // كراسات // طلاب // بنات // دولارات // أبواب // حافلات// أَطِبَّاءْ // صَناديِقْ

Answer	Question
معي أحدَ عشر قلماً	21) كَمْ قلماً مَعَكَ؟ 11
	22) كَمْ كتاباً في المكتبة؟ 1066
	23) كم كُرَّاسَةً في الصف؟ 204
	24) كم طالباً في المَدرسة؟ 503
	25) كم بِنْتاً في المدرسة؟ 201
	26) كم دولاراً في جَيْبِكَ؟ 5863
	27) كم باباً في الجامعة؟ 26
	28) كم حافِلَةً في الجامعة؟ 44
	29) كم مُمرضاً في المُسْتَشْفَى؟ 101
	30) كم صُنْدوقاً في المَخْزَنْ؟ 636

Reading and Writing a Six Digits Number in Arabic

Let us read the following number : 1589530

مِلْيون وَ خَمْسمِئة وَ تِسْعَة وَ ثَمانون أَلْف وَ خَمْسُمِئَة وَ ثَلاثُون.

Activity 18: Write the number phrase of the following Numerals in ARABic.

1. 4.569.020

----

2. 5.036.900

----

3. 2.030.690

----

4. 7.056.010

----

5. 2.060.100

----

6. 6.027.700

----

7. 6.102.030

----

8. 99.025.160

----

9. 2.706.030

----

10. 3.827.600

Activity 19: Listen to a series of numbers and write them down in Arabic digits in the space provided.

5.	4.	3.	2.	1.
10.	9.	8.	7.	6.
15.	14.	13.	12.	11.
20.	19.	18.	17.	16.

Activity 20: Listen to a series of numbers and write the English equivalent in the space provided.

5.	4.	3.	2.	1.
10.	9.	8.	7.	6.
15.	14.	13.	12.	11.
20.	19.	18.	17.	16.

Activity 21: Listen to a series of numbers and write the English equivalent in the space provided.

5.	4.	3.	2.	1.
10.	9.	8.	7.	6.
15.	14.	13.	12.	11.
20.	19.	18.	17.	16.

Passage 1: Introducing Yourself and Your Family

عـرِّف نفسَـكَ و عائِـلـتـكَ

اِسْمي چون، وُلِدْتُ في يَوْم تِسْعةَ عَشْرَ مِنْ شَهْر أُغْسْطُس مِنْ عام أَلْف وتِسْعُمِئَة وثَلاثـة وسِـتُّون. وُلِدْت في يَوْم الإثْنَيْـن.

أنا دَرَسْتُ هَنْدَسَة المِيكانِيكا في جامِعة ڤيرچينيا و تَخَرَجْتُ في عام أَلْف وَ ثَمانِمائة وسَبْعَة وثَمانون. أنا ضابِطٌ في الجَيْشِ الأَمْريكيّ. أَبي وَ أَخي أُسْتاذانِ في جامِعَة "بوسطن". وَ أَخي الأَصْغر طَبِيب وَ أُمِي رَبَّةُ بَيْتٍ.

عِندي ثَلاثَةُ أَبْناءٍ، وَلَدٌ واحِدٌ وَ اِبنَتانِ اِثْنتانِ. اِبْني عُمـرُهُ أَرْبَعُ وَ عِشْرون سَـنَة وَ يَعْمَلُ فِي مَتْجَر "بِستْ *باي*". اِبْنَتي الكُبْرى دَرَسَتْ الفِيزْياء فِي جامِعَة *أَرِيزُونا* وَ تَعْمَلُ فِي شَرِكَة كَبِيرَة وَ هِي مُتَزَوْجَة. و اِبْنَتي الصُّغْرى تَذْهبُ إِلى المَدْرَسَة الإعْدادِيَّة في مَدينَة "*فِينِكْس*".

أنا أَسْكُنُ في بَيْتٍ كَبيرٍ في مَدِينَة *فِينِكْس* بِـوِلايَة أريزُونا، البَيْت فِيهِ حَدِيقَةٌ كَبِيرَةٌ و أَشْجار بُرْتُقالٍ وَ تُفَّاحٍ. البَيْت فِيهِ ثَلاث غُرَفٍ وَ مَطْبَخٍ و حمَّـامَيْنِ.

في عُطْلَة نِهايَة الأُسْبوع، أَذْهَبُ إِلىَ السِّينِما مَعَ أُسْرَتِي.

Passage 1 Vocabulary List

1. Kids	أَبْناء	2. I was born	وُلِدْتُ
3. 2 daughters	اِبنَتَيْن	4. Month	شَهر
5. Store	مَتْجَر	6. Of/ from	مِنْ
7. Physics	الفِيزْياء	8. Year	عَام
9. She works	تَعْمَلُ	10. Engineering	هَنْدَسَة
11. Company	شَرِكَة	12. Mechanic	المِيكانِيكا
13. Married F.	مُتَزَوْجَة	14. I graduated	تَخَرَجْتُ
15. Garden	حَديقَة	16. Officer	ضابِطٌ
17. The eldest F.	الكُبْرَى	18. Army	الجَيْشِ
19. The youngest F.	الصُّغْرى	20. The youngest M.	الأَصْغر
21. Preparatory	الإعْدادِيَّة	22. Physician	طَبِيب
23. Trees	أَشْجار	24. House wife	رَبَّة بَيْت
25. 2 bathrooms	حمَّامَيْنِ	26. Kitchen	مَطْبَخ
27. End	نِهايَة	28. Vacation	عُطْلَة
29. Rooms	غُرَف	30. The week	الأُسْبوع

Activity 22: Create a passage about yourself or someone close to you following the EEI (Essential elements of instructions) in passage 1:

Lesson 12 Vocabulary List					
1.	**Hand**	يَدُ	33)	Nurse	مُمَرِّضٌ
2.	**Bath**	حَمَّامِ	34)	ear	أُذنٍ.f
3.	**Flower**	زَهْرَةُ	35)	Rabbit	أرْنبٌ
4.	**Basin**	حَوْضَ	36)	Apple	تُفَّاحَةً
5.	**Fly**	ذُبابَةٍ	37)	physician	طبيبٌ
6.	**Journalist**	صَحَفيٌّ	38)	Lemon	ليمونةٌ
7.	**Orange**	بُرْتُقالَةٍ	39)	SICK Person	مريضٌ
8.	**Bull**	ثَوْرٌ	40)	Glasses	نظَّارةً
9.	**Fox**	ثَعْلَبٍ	41)	Notebook	كُراسَةٍ
10.	**Island**	جَزيرَةٌ	42)	eye	عَيْنٌ.f
11.	**Research**	البَحْث	43)	Kid /s	طفل // أطْفالٍ
12.	**Kids**	أَبْناء	44)	Hospital	المُسْتَشْفَى
13.	**2 daughters**	اِبنَتيْن	45)	Storage	المَخْزَنْ
14.	**Store**	مَتْجَر	46)	Pocket	جَيْبِكَ
15.	**Physics**	الفِيزْياء	47)	Roaster	دِيك
16.	**She works**	تَعْمَلُ	48)	Chicken	دَجَاجَةً
17.	**Company**	شَرِكَة	49)	Story	قِصَّةً
18.	**Married F.**	مُتَزَوْجَة	50)	Friend	صَدِيق
19.	**Garden**	حَديقَة	51)	Year	سَنَةً
20.	**The eldest F.**	الكُبْرَى	52)	I was born	وُلِدْتُ
21.	**The youngest F.**	الصُّغْرى	53)	Month	شَهْر
22.	**Preparatory School**	المَدْرسة الإعْدادِيَّة	54)	Of/ from	مِنْ
23.	**Trees**	أَشْجار	55)	Year	عَام

24. **2 bathrooms**	حمَّامَيْنِ	56) Engineering	هَنْدَسَة
25. **End**	نِهايَة	57) Mechanic	المِيكانِيكا
26. **Rooms**	غُرَف	58) I graduated	تَخَرَجْتُ
27. **Kids**	أَبْناء	59) Officer	ضابِطٌ
28. **2 daughters**	اِبنَتَيْن	60) Army	الجَيْشِ
29. **Store**	مَتْجَر	61) The youngest M.	الأَصْغر
30. **Physics**	الفِيزْياء	62) Physician	طَبِيب
31. **Kitchen**	مَطْبَخ	63) House wife	رَبَّة بَيْت
32. **Vacation**	عُطْلَة	64) The week	الأُسْبوع

LESSON 13

Ordinal Numbers

الأَعْداد التَـرْتِيبيَّـة

	Masculine	Feminine
1st	الأَوَّل	الأُولَى
2nd	الثَّاني	الثَّانِيَة
3rd	الثَّالث	الثَّالِثَة
4th	الرَّابِع	الرَّابِعَة
5th	الخَامِس	الخَامِسَة
6th	السَّادِس	السَّادِسَة
7th	السَّابِع	السَّابِعَة
8th	الثَّامِن	الثَّامِنَة
9th	التَّاسِع	التَّاسِعَة
10th	العاشِر	العاشِرَة
11th	الحادي عَشَر	الإِحْدَى عَشْرَة
12th	الثاني عشر	الاثنا عشرة
13th	الثالث عشر	الثالثة عشرة
14th	الرابع عشر	الرابعة عشرة
15th	الخامس عشر	الخامسة عشرة
16th	السادس عشر	السادسة عشرة
17th	السابع عشر	السابعة عشرة
18th	الثامن عشر	الثامنة عشرة
19th	التاسع عشر	التاسعة عشرة
20th	العشرون	العشرون

Feminine	Masculine	
الحادِيَة والعشرون	الحادي والعشرون	21st
الثانِيَة والعشرون	الثاني والعِشرون	22nd
الثالثة والعشرون	الثالث والعشرون	23rd
الرابعة والعشرون	الرابع والعشرون	24th
الخامسة والعشرون	الخامس والعشرون	25th
السادسة والعشرون	السادس والعشرون	26th
السابعة والعشرون	السابع والعشرون	27th
الثامنة والعشرون	الثامن والعشرون	28th
التاسعة والعشرون	التاسع والعشرون	29th
الثلاثون	الثلاثون	30th
الحادية والثلاثون	الحادي والثلاثون	31st
الثانية والثلاثون	الثاني والثلاثون	32nd
الثالثة والثلاثون	الثالث والثلاثون	33rd
الرابعة والثلاثون	الرابع والثلاثون	34th
الخامسة والثلاثون	الخامس والثلاثون	35th
السادسة والثلاثون	السادس والثلاثون	36th
السابع والثلاثون	السابع والثلاثون	37th
الثامنة والثلاثون	الثامن والثلاثون	38th
التاسعة والثلاثون	التاسع والثلاثون	39th
الأربعون	الأربعون	40th
الخمسون	الخمسون	50th
الستون	الستون	60th
السبعون	السبعون	70th
الثمانون	الثمانون	80th
التسعون	التسعون	90th
المئة / المائة	المئة / المائة	100th

Ordinal Numbers in phrases		**Cardinal Numbers in phrases**	
M.	F.	F.	M.
الطالب الأوَّل	الطالبة الأُولَى	طالبة وَاحِدَة	طالب وَاحِدٌ
الثَّاني	الثَّانِيَة	طالبتان اِثْنَتَانِ	طالبان اِثْنَان
الثَّالث	الثَّالِثَة	ثَلاثَة طلاب	ثَلاثُ طالبات
الرَّابِع	الرَّابِعَة	أَرْبَعَة	أَرْبَعْ
الخَامِس	الخَامِسَة	خَمْسَة	خَمْسْ
السَّادِس	السَّادِسَة	سِتَّة	سِتْ
السَّابِع	السَّابِعَة	سَبْعَة	سَبْعْ
الثَّامِن	الثَّامِنَة	ثَمَانِيَة	ثَمَانْ
التَّاسِع	التَّاسِعَة	تِسْعَة	تِسْعْ
العاشِر	العاشِرَة	عَـشَرَة	عَـشَرْ
الطالب الحادي عَشَر	الطالبة الإِحْدَى عَشْرَة	إِحْدَى عَشْرَةَ أستاذة	أحدَ عَشَرَ أُسْتاذاً
الطالب الثاني عشر	الطالبة الاثنا عشرة	اثْنَتا عَشْرَةَ مُهَنْدِسَةً // اِثْنَتَيْ عَشْرَةَ	اثْنَا عَشَرَ مُهَنْدِسًا // اِثْنَي عَشَر
الثالث عشر	الثالثة عشرة	ثَلاثَ عَشْرَةَ مُدَرِّسَة	ثلاثةَ عَشَرَ طالبًا
الرابع عشر	الرابعة عشرة	أَرْبَعَ عَشْرَةَ قِصَّةً	أَرْبَعَةَ عَشَرَ كِتَابًا
الخامس عشر	الخامسة عشرة	خَمْسَ عَشْرَةَ سَاعَةً	خَمْسَةَ عَشَرَ يَوْمًا
السادس عشر	السادسة عشرة	سِتَّ عَشْرَةَ طالبة	سِتَّةَ عَشَرَ طالبا
السابع عشر	السابعة عشرة	سَبْعَ عَشْرَةَ سيارةً	سَبْعَةَ عَشَرَ قلماً
الثامن عشر	الثامنة عشرة	ثَمانِيَ عَشْرَةَ صَدِيقَةً	ثَمَانِيَةَ عَشَرَ صَدِيقًا
التاسع عشر	التاسعة عشرة	تِسْعَ عَشْرَةَ سَنَةً	تِسْعَةَ عَشَرَ يَوْماً
الطالب العشرون	الطالبة العشرون	عشرون طالبة	عشرون يوما

Expressing Time

الوَقْت

We use the form of ordinal numbers with hours, with one exception only, which is:

One o'clock.

How to ask for the time in Arabic?

What time is it now?	كَـمْ السَّـاعَة الآن؟

Expressing Time

One O'clock	السَّـاعَة الوَاحِدَة
Two O'clock	السَّـاعَة الثَّانِيَة
Three O'clock	السَّـاعَة الثَّالِثَة
Four O'clock	السَّـاعَة الرَّابِعَة
Five O'clock	السَّـاعَة الخامِسَة
Six O'clock	السَّـاعَة السَّادِسَة
Seven O'clock	السَّـاعَة السَّابِـعَة
Eight O'clock	السَّـاعَة الثَّامِـنَة
Nine O'clock	السَّـاعَة التاسِـعَة
Ten O'clock	السَّـاعَة العاشِـرَة
Eleven O'clock	السَّـاعَة الحادِيَـة عَشْرَة
Twelve O'clock	السَّـاعَة الثَّـانِـيَة عَشْرَة

Expressing the Time Past the Hour For **5 minutes**	
	السَّـاعَة العاشـِرَة و خَمْس دَقائِـق
Expressing the Time **Before** the Hours **5 Minutes**	
	السَّـاعَة العاشـِرة إلَّا خَمْس دَقـائِـق
Note: We must insert (less) إلَّا between the hours and the minutes	

Expressing the Time Past the Hour For

10 minutes

السَّــاعَة العاشِــرة **وَ** عَــشْــر دَقائِق

We must insert (and) و between the hour and the miniutes

Expressing the Time **Before** the Hours

10 Minutes

السَّــاعَة العاشِــرة **إلَّا** عَــشْــر دَقائِق

Note: We must insert (less) إلَّا between the hours and the minutes

In order to express the time when the big hand is pointing at 15, 20, 30, 40, & 45 We Must Learn These Words First	
Quarter	الـــرُّبْع
Third	الثُّــلْث
Half	النِّــصْــف

Now let us express the time using these 3 words (الربع // الثلث // النصف)	
	السَّاعة العاشِرة و الرُّبْع
	السَّاعة العاشِرة إلا الرُّبع
	الساعة الثامنة إلا الثُّــلْث
	الساعة الثامنة و الثُّــلْث
	الساعة الثــالثة و النِّصْــف

Expressing time when the big hand is pointing at: 25 & 35 minutes.

	الساعة الرابعة و النِّصف إلا خمس دقائق
	الساعة الرابعة و النِّصف و خَمْس دقائق

How to express AM and PM in Arabic?

AM	صَباحاً
PM	مَساءً
Noon	ظُهْراً
Afternoon	بَعْدَ الظُّهْر
After-Afternoon (Between 2-5)	عَصْراً

Activity 1: Express time in writing sown in the clocks below, the first one is done for you:

	السَّاعَة العَاشِرَة وَ عَشْر دَقائِق
	(1 ______________________________
	(2 ______________________________
	(3 ______________________________
	(4 ______________________________
	(5 ______________________________

Activity 2: Express time in writing shown in the clocks below:

	.1
	.2
	.3
	.4
	.5

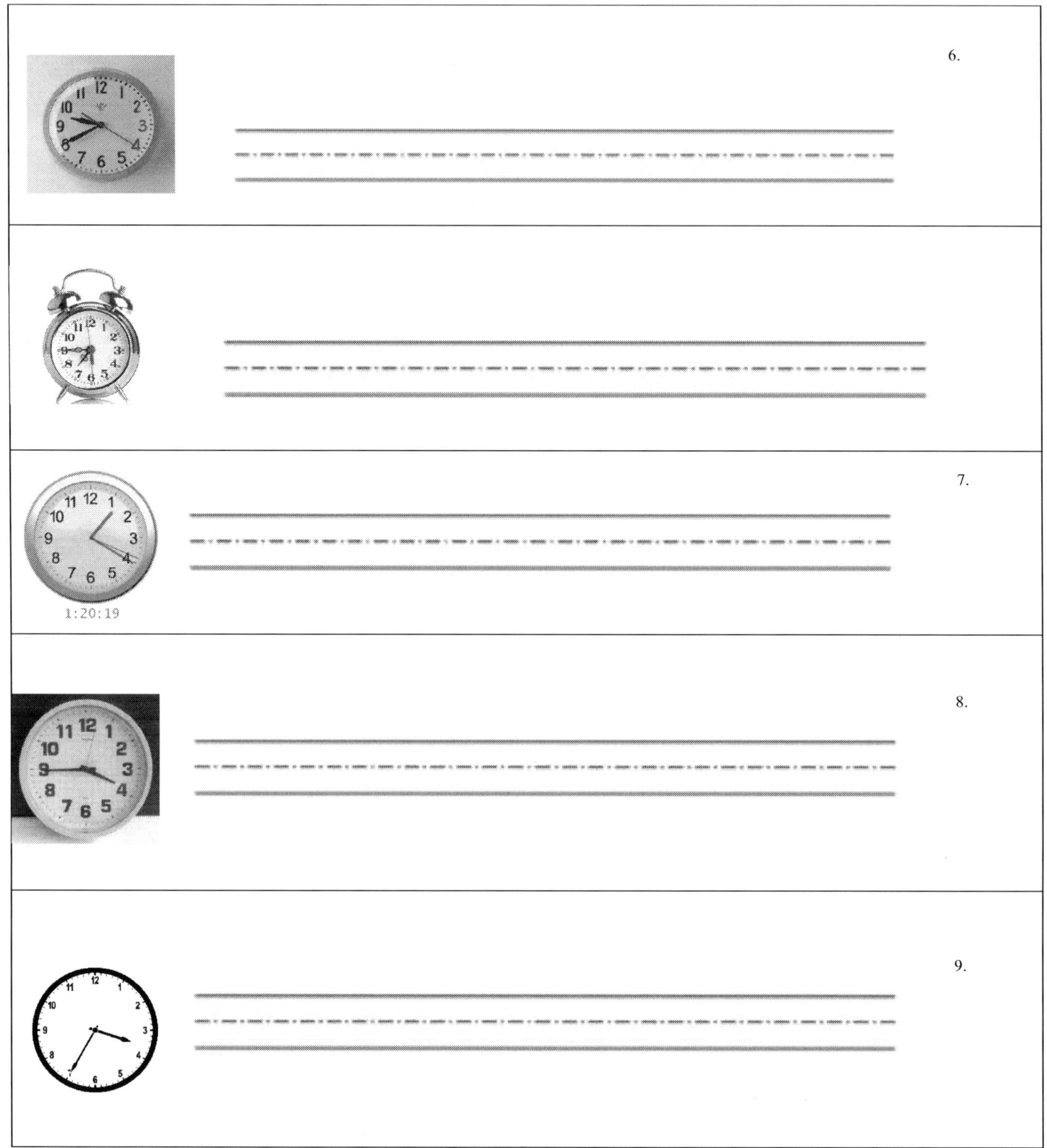
6.
7.
1:20:19
8.
9.

Different Types of Watches & Clocks	
 ساعَة يَدْ	 ساعَة حائِط
ساعَة مُنَــبِّه 	 ساعَة رَمْلِيَّة
 ساعَة إيقاف	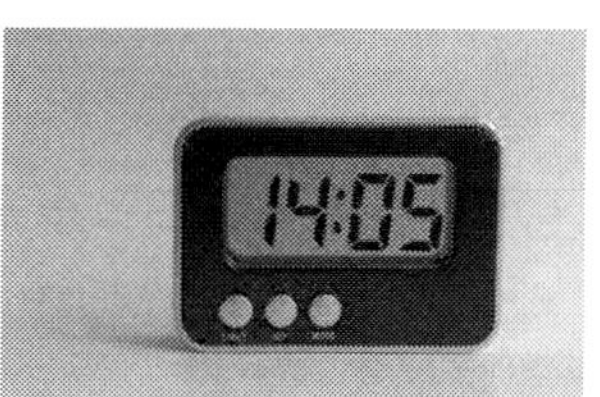 ساعَة رَقَمِيَة

Activity 3: Listen to a series of times and indicate the time mentioned in the table provided. The first one is done for you:

4.	3.	2.	1.
8.	7.	6.	5.
12.	11.	10.	9.
16.	15.	14.	13.
20.	19.	18.	17.
24.	23.	22.	21.
28.	27.	26.	25.
32.	31.	30.	29.
36.	35.	34.	33.
40.	39.	38.	37.

Activity 4: Listen to a series of times and indicate the time mentioned in the table provided. The first one is done for you:

4.	3.	2.	1.
8.	7.	6.	5.
12.	11.	10.	9.
16.	15.	14.	13.
20.	19.	18.	17.
24.	23.	22.	21.
28.	27.	26.	25.
32.	31.	30.	29.
36.	35.	34.	33.
40.	39.	38.	37.

Activity 5: Pretend that this is your daily schedule, record the time in each of the following sentences, then share you schedule with your classmate:

أذهبُ إلى الجَامِعَة في السَّاعَة ....
أذهبُ إلى المَطْعَم في السَّاعَة ....
أذهبُ إلى المَرْكَـز الرِيَّـاضِيّ في السَّاعَة ....
أَعودُ إلى المَنْـزِل في السَّاعَـة ....
أَبدأُ المُذَاكَـرَة في السَّاعَة ....
أذهبُ إلى النَـوْم في السَّـاعَة ....

Dialogue 16: An invitation

دَعْـوَة

مُصْطَفَى	أَهلاً أَحْمَد، مَرحباً. هَلْ تَذْهَبُ مَعي إِلىَ المَتْـجَر في المَـساء.
أحمد	في أَيِّ سَاعَة بِـالْمَساء؟
مصطفى	في السَّاعَة السَّادِسَة مَساءً.
أحمد	آسِـف، سَأَذْهَبُ إِلىَ بَيْت أَخي مَعَ زوَجتي في السَّاعَة السَّـادِسَـة و النِّـصْـف مَساءً.
مصطفى	هَلْ تَذْهَبُ مَعي غَداً؟
أحمد	نَعَم، سَأَذْهَبُ مَعكَ غَداً. في أَيِّ ساعَة؟
مصطفى	في نَـفْـسِ الـوَقْـت.
أحمد	تَمـام، اِتَـفَـقْـنـا.
مصطفى	إِلىَ اللِّـقاء غَـداً
أحمد	مَعَ السَّلامَة و إلى الِّـلـقـاء.

Communicative Activity : In pairs, role play the dialogue with your class partner, personalized it to your experience.

Dialogue 16: Vocabulary			
1. Same time	نَفْـسِ الوَقْـت	6. Store	المَتْـجَر
2. Perfect	تَمام	7. Which	أَيِّ
3. We agreed	اِتَّـفَـقْـنـا	8. Tomorrow	غَداً
4. Until we meet	إِلَى اللِّـقاء	9. Evening	المَساء
5. Sorry	آسِـف/ ة	10. Safety	السَّلامة

Write- Dialogue 16

Weather

الطَّـقْـس

Seasons	الفصول
فَصْل الشّـتاء	فَصْل الـرَّبيع

فَصْل الصَّـيْـف	فَصْل الخَـرِيف

فصل / فصول

Seasons	المَـواسِـم
1. Pilgrimage season	مَوْسِم الحَجْ
2. Harvest season	مَوْسِم الحَصاد
3. Holiday seasons	مَوْسِم الأعْياد
4. Tourism season	مَوْسِم السِّياحَة
موسم / مواسم	

Holidays	
Holiday, Feast	عِـيد //أَعْياد Plural
Birthday	عِيد مِيلاد
New Year's	رَأْس السَّنَة
Valentine's Day	عِيد الحُب
Easter/ Resurrection Sunday Or Passover	عِيد القِيامَة
	عِيد الفِصْح
Independence Day	عِيد الاستقلال
Thanksgiving	عِـيد الشُّكْر
Christmas	عِيد المِيلاد
New Year's Eve	لَيلة رأْس السَّنة
Eid Al-Adha	عِيد الأَضْحَى
Eid Al-Fitr	عِيد الفِطْر
Sham Al-Nesim	شَمّ النَّسيم

Dialogue 17: How Is Weather?

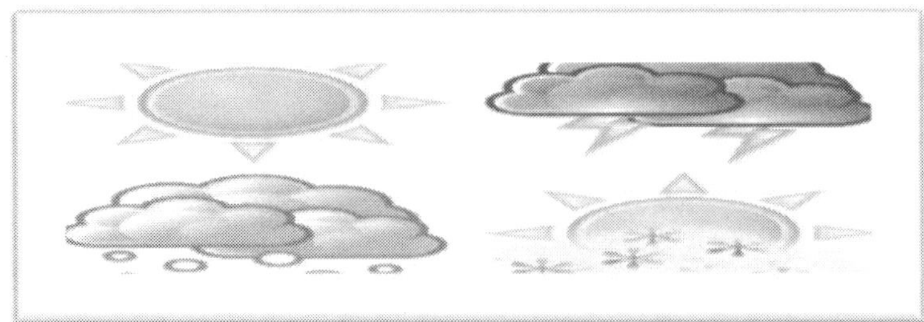

حُسام	أَلُو، مَرْحباً يا أَحْمَد، كَـيْـفَ حَالُـكَ الْيَـوْم؟
أحمد	أَهْلاً يا حُسام. أنا بِخَـيْـر و الحَمْـدُ لِـلَّه.
حسام	هَـلْ وَصَلْتَ إلى مَدِينَة " سان دييجو"؟
أحمد	نَعَم، وَصَلْـتُ أَمْـسْ، في السَّاعَة السَّابِعَة و النِّصْف مَساءً.
حسام	حَمْـداً لِـلَّه عَلى سَلامَـتِـكَ. و كَيْـفَ الطَّـقْـسُ هُـنَـاك؟
أحمد	الطَّقسُ هُـنا مُعْـتَـدِل جِداً، و دَرَجَـة الحَـرَارَة سَبْعـون فِهْرِنْـهايْت.
حسام	هَذا طَـقْسٌ رَائِع! الطَّقسُ هُـنا في "شيكاجو" بَـارِدْ جِـداً!
أحمد	كَـمْ دَرَجَـة الحَـرَارَة عِـنْـدَكَ؟
حسام	درجة الحرارة هُـنا حَوَالَيْ اِثْـنَـانِ و ثَـلاثون دَرَجَةً فِهرنهايت.
أحمد	هَـل هذه دَرجة الحَرارة العُـظْـمَى أَمْ الصُّـغْـرَى؟
حسام	هَـذِه دَرَجة الحَـرارة الصُّـغْـرَىَ!
أحمد	اِنْتَقِل إلىَ هُـنـا يَـا صَـديـقِـي!

Dialogue 17: Vocabulary			
2) To Arrive	وَصَـلَ	1) Praise be to God for your safety	حَمْداً لِلَّه عَلى سَلامَتِـك
4) yesterday	أَمْسْ	3) Temperature	دَرَجَة الحَرارَة
6) Weather	الطَّـقْـسْ	5) Amazing	رائع
8) Moderate	مُعْـتَـدِل	7) Approximately	حوالي
10) Very	جِداً	9) Highest temperature	دَرَجَة الحَرارَة العُـظْمَى
12) To move	اِنْـتَـقِـل	11) Lowest temperature	دَرَجَة الحَرارَة الصُّغْـرى
14) sunny	مُشْمِس	13) foggy	ضَبابِـيّ
16) snowy	مُثْلِج	15) rainy	ماطِر
18) windy	عاصِف	17) stormy	عاصِف
20) Rainbow	قوس قزح	19) cloudy	غائِم
22) Clear	صافـي	21) thunderstorm	عاصفة رعدية
24) wind	رياح	23) Tornado	إعصار

Write Dialogue 17

Activity 6: After reading dialogue 1, answer the following questions in English:

1. What is the temperature in San Diego?

2. What is the temperature in Chicago?

3. Who was traveling to San Diego? And When did he arrive?

Activity 7: Express the temperature in your city in the different seasons, in the space provide below.

-- -- -- --	.1
-- -- -- --	.2
-- -- -- --	.3
-- -- -- -- --	.4

Cardinal Directions

الإتـِّـجـاهـات

Activity 8: Draw The Direction That Matches Each Word

	1. North	الشَّـمَال
	2. South	الجَـنوب
	3. East	الشَّـرْق
	4. West	الغَـرْب
	5. Northwest	الشَّـمال الشَّـرْقِيّ
	6. Southeast	الجَـنوب الشَّـرْقِيّ
	7. Southwest	الجَـنـوب الغَـرْبِيّ
	8. Northeast	الشَّـمال الغَـرْبِيّ

Activity 9: Expressing Weather & Forecast

دَرَجَة الحرَارَة اليَوْم فِي شَمال وِلايَة نِيفادا خَمْسٌ وَ عِشْرون فِهْرِنْهايْت، الطَّقْسُ بارِد جِداً، هذا فَصْلُ الشِّتاء وَ هَذا شَهْرُ يَنايِر

دَرَجَة الحرَارَة اليَوْم في جَنوب وِلايَة تِكْساس، ثَمانٍ وَ تِسْعون، الطَّقْسُ حار جِداً، هذا فَصْلُ الصَّيفِ وَ هَذا شَهْر يُوليو.

دَرَجَة الحرَارَة اليَوْم في غرب مَدينَة سَان دِييجو، سَبْعُ وَ سِتُّون فِهْرِنْهايْت، الطَّقْسُ اليَوْم مُعْتَدِل، هذا فَصْلُ الرَّبيع وَ هَذا شَهْر إبْريل

اليَوْمُ، في شمال وِلاية وَاشِنْطُن، الطَّقْسُ مُمْطِر وَ غائِم وَ هُناك ضَباب [1] كَثِيف فِي الصَّباح البَاكِر[2]

[1]Dense, [2]Early

Activity 10: You are listening to the radio and you find and Arabic news station describing international weather conditions. Listen to the segments and write the name of the city, then write the adjective describing the weather condition, then write down the temperature associated with each city

Temperature lowest	Temperature highest	Weather condition	City name
درجة الحرارة الصُّغْرى	دَرَجَة الحَرارة الكُبْرى	حالَة الطَّقْس	إِسْم المَدينَة

Activity 11: Introduce yourselves, giving your name, where you are from, what the weather is like in your home state in each of the four seasons, and what the temperature there is today

اسمي چون أنا من ولاية .... ، الطقس ....

هناك في فصل .... و .... في فصل

....

....

....

....

....

....

Dialogue 18: Talking With Mom Over The Phone!

الأُم	آلو، أَهلاً يا هـاني يا حَبـيـبـِي.
هاني	أهلاً يا ماما، كَيْفَ حَالُـكِ اليَـوْم؟
الأم	أنــا بِخَـيْـر يا حَـبيبِي، كَيْفَ الطَّـقـسُ عِـنْـدَكَ فـي مَدينة "سـان فرانسيسكو"؟
هاني	الطَّـقـس هُـنا مُعْـتَـدِل جِـداً، لَـيْـسَ حـار و لَـيْـسَ بارِد!
الأُم	هذا رائِع، الطَّقسُ هُـنا في" شيكاجو" بارِد جِداً.
هاني	يا أُمِّي، فَـصْـل الرَّبيع بَـعْـد عَـشْـرَة أَيَّـــام! اليَومْ هو الثَّـاني عَـشَر مِن شَـهْـر مَـارِس!

Dialogue 18: Vocabulary list

1.	Weather	الطَّـقـس	2.	Darling M.	حَبـيـبـِي
3.	NOT	لَـيْـسَ	4.	Moderate	مُعْـتَـدِل
5.	Cold	بارِد	6.	Hot	حـار
7.	After	بـَعْـد	8.	Wonderful	رائِع
9.	Spring	الرَّبيع	10.	Days	أَيَّـــام

Write Dialogue 18

الأُم

هاني

الأم

هاني

الأُم

هاني

Negation of The Equational Sentence

The use of لَـيْـسَ

لَيْس is a verb	**Example** رامي في البيت رامي لَيْـسَ في البيت
ليسis a combination of لا + The unused أيْس meaning "being" or "existence." Thus, the verb ليس means "not to be" or "is not."	
The verb is most often used in order to negate an equational sentence.	
It conjugates Only in the past tense, even though it negates a nominal sentence in the present tense, It takes a direct object.	

Conjugations Of لَيْسَ

We add the same suffixes to it that we use when we conjugate any verb in the past tense.

Of course, we will only have present tense meaning with ليس. Enjoy.

Plural Pronouns		Singular Pronouns	
لَسْنا	نَحْنَ	لَسْتُ	أنــا
لَسْتُم	أنْــتُـم	لَسْتَ	أنْتَ
لَسْتُنَّ	أنْــتُنَّ	لَـسْتِ	أنْتِ
لَيْسوا	هُـمْ	لَـيْسَ	هُوَ
لَسْنَ	هُـنَّ	لَـيْسَـت	هِيَ
لَيْسا	هما	لستما	أنتما
لَيْستا	هما	لستما	أنتما

Activity 3: Negate the following sentences using the proper conjugation of ليس

1) أنا من ولاية نيومكسيكو

2) الطقس اليوم بارد جداً في مدينة رينو

3) مدينة ساكرامنتو بعيدة من مدينة سان فرانسيسكو

4) في البيت خمس غُرف

5) ابنتي اسمها هند

6) عندي ستَّة بَنات

7) نعم، الشَّقة قَرِيبَة مِنْ هُـنا

8) اليوم، درجة الحرارة العُظْمى واحِدٌ وُ تِسْعون فِهْرِنْهايت

Lesson 13 - Vocabulary List

Hour /s	ساعة // ساعات	.1
Minute	دقيقة // دقائق	.2
Second	ثانية // ثواني	.3
Moment	لحظة // لحظات	.4
Time (As A General Concept)	زمان // أزمنة	.5
Time	وقت // أوقات	.6
(Countable Unit For "Time) ; As In "Three Times, Four Times," Etc.)	مَرَّة // مَرَّات	.7
Century	قَـرْن //قـرون	.8
Decade	حِقْبَة	.9
Year	سَنَة// سَنوات	.10
Week	أُسْبوع //أَسَابيع	.11
Day	يَوْم //أيّام	.12
Sunrise	شُروق الشَّمْس	.13
Noon	ظُهْر	.14
Afternoon	بَعْد الظُّهر	.15

English	Arabic	No.
Midnight	مُنْتَصَف اللَّيْل	.16
Night	ليلة // ليالي	.17
Dawn	فَجْر	.18
Before	قَبْل	.19
After	بَعْد	.20
Then	ثُـمَّ	.21
Until	حَتَّى	.22
Now	الآن	.23
The Day Before Yesterday	أول أمس	.24
Yesterday	أمس	.25
Last Night	ليلة أمس	.26
Today	اليوم	.27
Tomorrow	غداً	.28
The Day After Tomorrow	بَعْدَ الغَد	.29
Last (Week)	الأُسْبوع المَاضِي	.30
Next (Week)	الأُسْبوع القادِم	.31

LESSON 14

Daily Meals

الوَجَـبات اليَوْمِـيَّة

وَجْبَـةُ الـفُـطُـورِ

وَجْبَـةُ الـغَـدَاءِ

وَجْبَـةُ الـعَـشَـاءِ

Fruits and Vegetables

فَـواكِه و خُضْـراوات

	عِشْ الغُراب		قَرْنَبيط
	جَزَرْ		ذُرَة
	فِلْفِل أَحْمَر	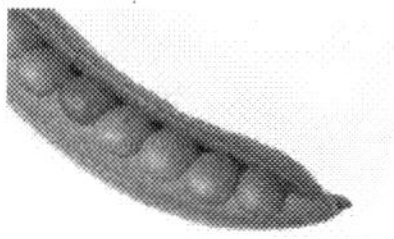	بازِلاَّء
	بَنْجَر		بْروكْلي
	حُمُص		فاصوليا
	خِيَار		طَماطِم
	كمثرى		قرنبيط

جوز هند		توت أزرق	
كرز		توت أسود	
فراولة		توت أحمر	
أناناس		عنب أحمر	
خوخ		عنب أخضر	
برقوق	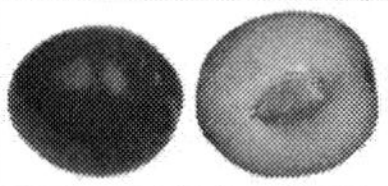	مشمش	
تين		موز	
برتقال		يوسفي	
كرنب اخضر	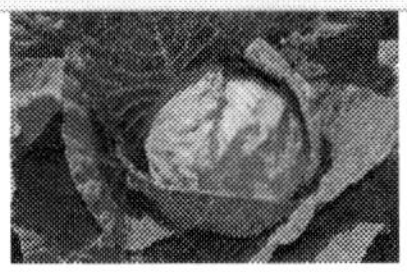	خرشوف	

	بطاطس		كرنب احمر
	بطاطا		فجل حمر
	كوسة		قرع
	ثَوْمْ		بصل
	بقدونس		باذنجان
	كزبرة خضراء	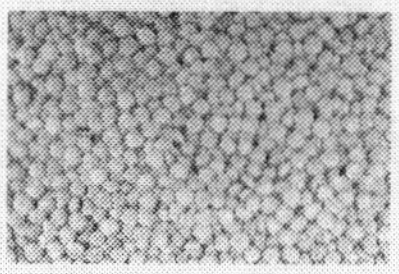	عدس
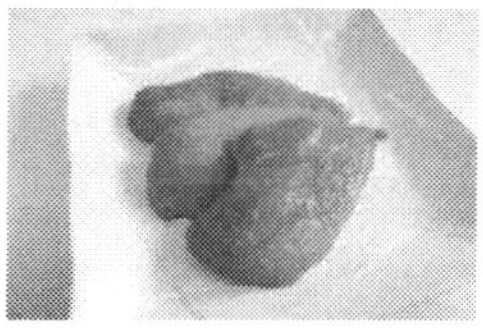	دَجاج		لَحْمْ
	بَيْضْ	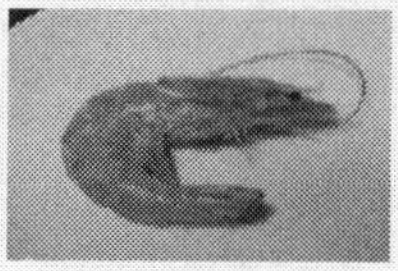	جَمْبَرِي

قَواقِعْ		سالامون	
جَنْزَبِيل	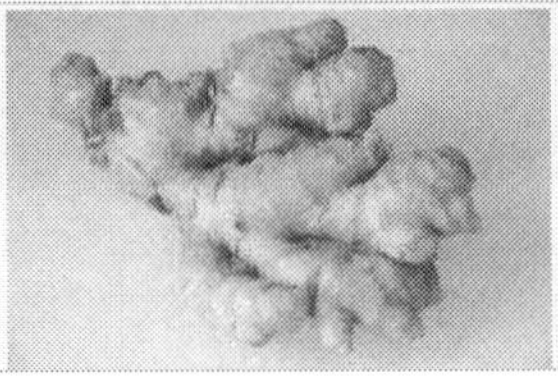	دَقِيقْ	
سَكَّر		تُونَة	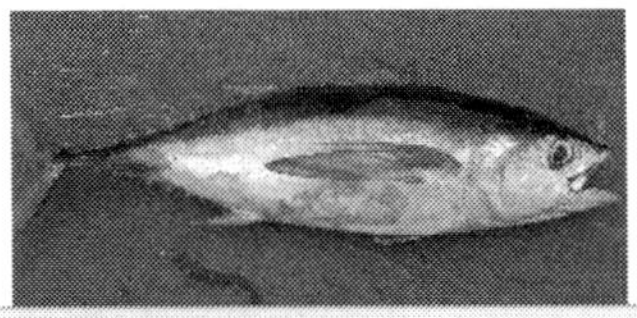
ملح	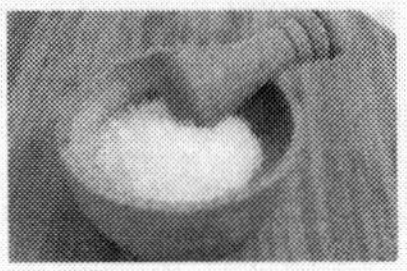	بسطرمة	
قمح		شعير	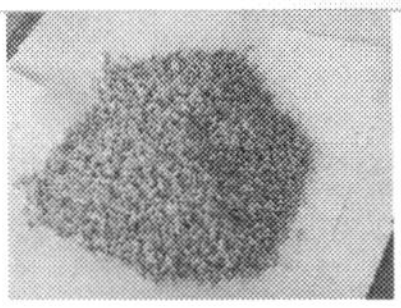
مَانْجو		شَمَّام	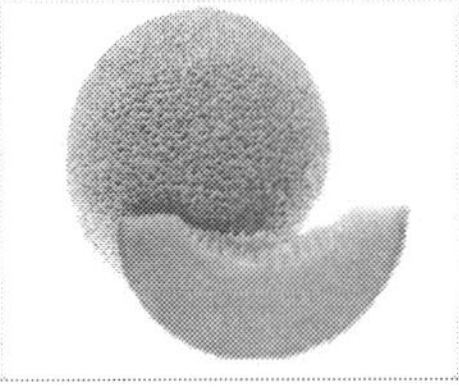
كِيوِي		رمان	
خس		شوفان	

نَبِيذ
بِيرَة
عَصِير
حليب
تَمْر
زبادي

Plates

أَطْـباق

طَبَقْ

طَبَق بَـيْـض معَ خُبْز

كَبابْ

طبق حُمُّص

طبق طَحِينَة

طبق حَلَوِيات مُشَكَّلْ

صِينِيَّة بَسْبوسَة

طبق ورَقْ عِنَب مَحْشِيّ

طَبَقْ بَقْلاوَة

Activity 1: Create a list of your favorite food in each meal in the table below:

وجبة العشاء	وجبة الغداء	وجبة الفطور

Dialogue 19: At the restaurant

في المَطْعَم

النادل	مرحباً و أهلاً وسهلاً
أمير	شكراً، نريدُ مائِدَةً كَبيرةً بِالقُـرْبِ مِنْ النَّافِـذَة.
النادل	تَفَضَّل مِنْ هُـنا، مِن فَضلِك.
	هَذِهِ قَائِمَةُ الطَّعام، هَـل تَـشْرَبون شَيئاً؟
	مَاءْ أو عَـصيرْ أو أيَّ مَشْروبٍ آخَرْ؟
أمير	مَاء بِدون ثَـلْجْ لـي، مِنْ فَضْلِك.
نادية	أنا أُريد عَصير بُرتُقال، مِن فَضْلِك. و عَصير تُفَّاح لِلأَوْلاد.
النادل	بِـكُـلِ سُرورٍ، لَحَـظاتٌ و أَعـودُ بِالمَشْروباتِ.

بَعْـدَ قَـلِيـل

النادل	هَذِهِ هِيَ المَشْروبات. هَل سَـتَـطْـلُبون الطَّعامَ الآن؟
أمير	نَعم، أنا أُريدُ طَـبَقْ كَبابْ مَشْـوِيّ مَعَ السَّلَطَة الخَـضْراء، شُـكراً.
نادية	و أنا أُريدُ نِـصْـف دَجَاجَة مَـشْـوِيَّة مَعَ البَـطاطِـس المَـقْـلِيَّة، و نَـفْسُ الشيء لِـلأَوْلاَد الـثَّـلاثَـة، مِـن فَـضْـلِـك.
النادل	حَـاضِر، الطَّعامُ سَيكون جَاهِـز في خِلال رُبْعِ سَاعَة.

بَعد حَوالَيّ رُبْعِ سَاعَة

الـنادل	هَذِهِ أَطْباق الطَّعام

أمير	شُكراً

بَعَد حَواليّ نِصْف سَاعَة

النَّادِل	هل تُحِبُون أيّ حَلَويات أو فَاكِهَة؟
أمير	نَعم، مِن فَضْلِك، أنا أُريدُ قِطْعَةً مِن كَعْكَة الشُّوكولاتَة.
نادية	أنا أريدُ فِنْجان مِن القَهْوَةِ و قِطْعَتَيْنِ مِن البَقْلاوَة لِلأَوْلاد.
النادل	حَاضِر، سأُحضرُ الطَّلَبات، حَالاً.

بَعد قَلِيل

النادل	تَفَضَّلوا، هَذِهِ هِيَ أطْباقُ الحَلِوياتِ و القَهْوة.

بَعد ثُلْث سَاعة

أمير	مِن فَضْلِك أُريدُ الحِساب. كم المبلغ ؟
النادل	تَفَضَّل، المبلغ مِئَة و ثَلاثَة و سَبعون جُنَيْه.

بَعد قَليل

أمير	تفضل الحساب، و شُكراً عَلىَ الخِدْمَة المُمْتازَة.
النادل	عَفْواً و إِلىَ زِيارَة قَرِيبَة لِلمَطْعَم.
أمير	بِكُلِ تأكِيدٍ
النادل	مَعَ السَّلامَة

Write Dialogue 19: At the restaurant

النادل

أمير

النادل

أمير

نادية

النادل

النادل

أمير

نادية

النادل

الـنـادل

أمير

الـنَّـادِل

أمير

نادية

النادل

النادل

أمير

النادل

أمير

النادل

أمير

النادل

Dialogue 19: Vocabulary

1. Ice	ثَـلْج	22. We want	نريد
2. Juice	عَصير	23. Table	مائِدَة
3. For the kids	لِلأَوْلاد	24. Near by	بِالقُـرْبِ
4. Will all happiness (pleasure)	بِـكُـل سُرور	25. List	قائِمَة
5. Moments	لَحَـظات	26. Food	الطَّعام
6. I return	أعـود	27. You P. Drink	تَـشْرَبون
7. You P. will request	سَـتَـطْـلُبون	28. Thing	شَيءْ
8. Now	الآَن	29. Water	مَاء
9. Plate	طَـبَق	30. Or	أو
10. Salad	السَّلَطَة	31. Juice	عَـصير
11. Fried	المَـقْـلِيَّة	32. Any	أيّ
12. Same thing	نَـفْسْ الشيء	33. A drink	مَشْروب
13. Ready	جَاهِـز	34. Else / other	آخَر
14. During	خِلال	35. Without	بِدون
15. Approximately	حَواليّ	36. Desserts	حَلَوِيات
16. Little bit	قَليل	37. Fruits	فَاكِهَة
17. Service	الخِـدْمَة	38. Piece	قِـطْعَة
18. The excellent	المُمْتازَة	39. Cake	كَعْـكَة
19. The bill / Account	الحِـساب	40. Cup	فِـنْجان
20. Visit	زِيارَة	41. Coffee	القَهْـوَة
21. With all certainty	بِـكُـل تَأكِيد	42. Baclava	البَـقْلاوَة
22. Right away	حَالاً	43. I will bring	سأُحضر

Verb to Love / Like (Geminate verb: Second and third letters of the verb root, are the same)	

Past ماضي				
Dual	حَبَبْنَا	نَحْنُ	حَبَبْتُ	أنا
أنتما حَبَبْتُمَا	حَبَبْتُمْ	أَنْتُم	حَبَبْتَ	أنتَ
أنتما حَبَبْتُمَا	حَبَبْتُنَّ	أَنْتُنَّ	حَبَبْتِ	أنتِ
هما حَبَّا	حَبُّوا	هُمْ	حَبَّ	هُوَ
هما حَبَّتَا	حَبَبْنَ	هُنَّ	حَبَّتْ	هِيَ

Presentمضارع				
Dual	نُحِبُّ	نَحْنُ	أُحِبُّ	أنا
أنتما تَحِبَّانِ	تُحِبُّونَ	أَنْتُم	تُحِبُّ	أنتَ
أنتما تَحِبَّانِ	تُحْبِبْنَ	أَنْتُنَّ	تُحِبِّينَ	أنتِ
هما يَحِبَّانِ	يُحِبُّونَ	هُمْ	يُحِبُّ	هُوَ
هما تَحِبَّانِ	يُحْبِبْنَ	هُنَّ	تُحِبُّ	هِيَ

Negating the Present Tense	
by using لا	
أنا لا أُحِبُّ	أنا أُحِبُّ
I don't like / Love	I Like / love

Activity 2: Use all the food items you have learned in this lesson, pretend that you are at a restaurant with your friends, discuss what each of you would like to eat. In the space below, write down what you and your friends have decided to order:

Activity 3: Pretend that you are at restaurant in Cairo, role play with your class partner, you are the client and your partner is the waiter. Inquire about different food types for any of the 3 essential meals. You may refer to all the food items and plates you have learned in this lesson:

Dialogue 20: At the Grocery

عِـنْـدَ البَـقّـال

نادِيَة	صباحُ الخيْر، هَـلْ عِـندكَ لَـحْم بَقَريّ؟
البقال	لا، و لَـكِـن عِـنْدي لَحْم جـامـُوس.
نادية	هَـل عِـندكَ بَيْض؟
البقال	نَعم، عِـندي بَيْض.
نادية	هل عِنْدكَ فَـراوْلَة؟
البقال	لا آسِـفْ، لَيْس عِـندي فراولة. عِندي تُـوتْ أحْمَر.
نادية	هل عِـنـدك لَبَن و حليب ؟
البقال	نَعم عندي لَبَـن كَـامِـل الدَّسَـمْ و لكن ليس عندي حليب.
نادية	كَمْ سِـعْـر كيلو اللَّبَن؟ أُريدُ ثلاثةُ كِيلووَات.

البقال	السِّعْـر خَـمْـس جُـنَـيْـهات لِلكِيلو.
نادية	كَـم المَبْـلَغ الكُـلـيّ؟
البقال	خَمْسة عَشرة جُنَيْه
نادية	تَـفَضَل مِـئَة جُـنَـيْه، كَـم البَـاقِـي؟
البقال	الباقي خَمس و ثَمانـون جُـنَـيْـه، تَـفَـضَلي و شُـكراً لكِ.
نادية	شكرا لكَ، مَـعَ السَّلامَة.
البقال	مَـع السَّلامَة.

Dialogue 20 Vocabulary			
8. Price	سِـعْـر	1. Cow meat	لَحْم بَقَريّ
9. Kilos	كِيلووَات	2. No	لا
10. The amount	المَبْـلَغ	3. But	لَـكِـن
11. Total	الكُـلـيّ	4. Buffalo	جاموس
12. The remainder	البَـاقِـي	5. Sorry	آسِـفْ
13. With safety / Good Bye	مَـعَ السَّلامَة.	6. Full /Complete	كَـامِـل
14. How much	كَمْ	7. Fat	الدَّسَـمْ

Write Dialogue 20

نادِيَة

البقال

نادية

البقال

نادية

البقال

نادية

البقال

نادية

البقال

نادية

البقال

نادية

البقال

نادية

البقال

Activity 4: Your mom has left you a message asking you to buy some food items from the supermarket. Listen to her message and create a list for the items.

المَجْموع Total	ثَمَن Price	بَنْد Item

Classroom Communication

يا أستاذ/ة، عندي مَوْعِدٌ مَع الطَّبيب، غداً.

Professor, tomorrow I have an appointement at the doctor.

Activity 5: Answer the following questions In Arabic:

1. ما اسمك؟

2. ما يوم ميلادك؟

3. هل أنت متزوج؟

4. و هل عندك أولاد؟ كم ولدا ,كم بنتا عندك؟

5. في أي مدينة ولِدت؟

6. كم غرفة في بيتك؟

7. هل عندك سيارة؟ ما لون سيارتك؟

8. هل عندك حاسوب؟

9. هل أنت طالب؟ ماذا تدرس؟

10. هل سافرت في عطلة الصيف؟ أين سافرت؟

11. هل تعمل؟ أين؟

Lesson 14 Vocabulary List

1. Food	طَـعَامْ / أَطْـعِـمَة (p)	1. To Eat	أَكَـلَ – يَأْكُـل
2. Foods	مَأْكُولاتْ	2. To Drink	شَـرِبَ – يَشْرَبْ
3. Meal	وَجْـبَة // وَجَـبـاتْ	3. To Cook	طَبَخَ - يَطْبُخ
4. Restaurant	مَـطْـعَـم /مَطاعِـم	4. To Bake (Esp. Bread)	خَبَزَ – يَخْبِزْ
5. Coffee Shop	مَـقْـهَـى	5. Soda Water /Sparkling Water	ماء الصودا / مِياه غازِيَّة
6. Waiter	نَـادِلْ	6. To Stir	حَـرَّكَ - يُحَرِّك
7. Breakfast Meal	وَجْـبَة فُـطـور	7. To Mix	خَلَطَ - يَخْلِطْ
8. Lunch Meal	وَجْـبَة غَـداء		
9. Dinner Meal	وَجْـبَة عَـشاءْ	8. To Pour	صَبَّ - يَصُب
10. To Have Breakfast	فَـطَـر – يَـفْـطِـر		سَكَبَ - يَسْكُب
11. To Have Lunch	تَـغَـدَّى – يتغـدى	9. To Boil (Water)	غَلَىَ - يَغْلِي
12. To Have Dinner	تَعَـشَّى - يتعشَّى	10. To Boil (Food)	سَلَقَ - يَسْلِق
13. Recipe	وَصْـفَة / وَصَفَات(p)	11. To Boil Over (To Overflowing)	فَارَ - يَفُور
14. Ingredient	مِقْدار // مَقادِير(p)	12. To Burn, Be Scorched	شَاطَ - يَشِيط
15. Can	عُلْبَة / عَـلَـبْ(p)	13. To Dissolve	ذَوَّبَ - يُذَوِّب
16. Box	صُنْدوق/ صَـناديق (p)	14. To Melt	سَـيَّـحَ – يُسَـيِّح
17. Fry pan	مقلاة	15. To Sprinkle, Scatter	نَـشَـر – يَـنْـشُـر
18. Hungry (Hunger)	جَـائِـع		رَشَّ – يَـرُشُّ
19. Thirsty (Thirst)	عَـطْـشان	16. To Add (To)	أَضَافَ - يُضِيف
20. Full X Hungry (From Eating)	شَـبْـعـان x جوعان	17. To Heat Up	سَخَّنَ - يُسَخِّن
21. Mango	مَانْجُـو	18. To Grease S.T. (With)	دَهَـنَ – يَـدْهِـن

22. Olive	زَيْـتون	19. Fig	تـيـن
23. Cutlery	أَدَوات المَائِـدَة	20. Yoghurt	زَبادِي / لَـبَنْ رائِبْ
24. Fork	شَـوْكَـة	21. Milk	حَـلـيب or لَـبَـنْ
25. Spoon	مِلْعَـقَة	22. Salt	مَـلْـحْ
26. Knife	سِـكِّـين	23. Pepper	فِـلْـفِـلْ
27. Plate	طَـبَـقْ	24. Spices	بَـهارات
28. Cup	كُـوب	25. Oil	زَيْـتْ
29. Coffee	قَـهْـوَة	26. Tasty / Delicious	لَـذِيذْ
30. Tea	شَـايْ	27. Soup	حِـساء
31. Bitter	مُـر	28. Salad	سَـلَـطَـة
32. Salty	مَـالِـح	29. French Fries	بَـطاطِس مَقْلِيَّة
33. Spicy	حَـار	30. Juice [Sg]	عَـصِـيـر
34. Fruit	فَـاكِـهَـة	31. Wine	نَـبـيـذْ
35. Vegetables	خُـضْـرَاواتْ	32. Beer	جِـعَـة / بِيرَة
36. Apple [Sg]	تُـفَّـاحَة	33. Orange	بُـرْتُـقالَـة
37. Chocolate	شُـوكُـولاتَـة	34. Strawberry	فَـراوْلَـة
38. Pie [Sg]	فَـطـيرَة	35. Banana	مَوْزَة
39. Cake [Sg]	كَـعْـكَة	36. Cucumbers	خِـيـار
40. Biscuits [Pl]	بَـسْـكَـوِيت	37. Meat	لَحْـم

41. Ice-Cream	آيس كِريم or بوظة	38. Ham	لحم خَـنْـزِير
42. Chicken	دَجَـاجْ	39. Lamb	لَحْـم ضَأْن
43. Parsley	بَقْـدونِـس	40. Fish	سَـمَـك/ أَسْمَاك(p)
44. Tomato	طَـماطِـم	41. Onion	بَـصَـلْ
45. Pot	طَـنْجَـرَة	42. Garlic	ثـَوْمْ
46. stove	فُـرْنْ	43. Kitchen	مطبخ
47. Menu	قَائِـمَـة طَـعَام	44. Delivery service	خِـدْمَة تَـوْصِيـل
48. Oat	شوفان	45. Lettuce	خس
49. Item	بَـنْـد	46. Total	المَجْموع
50. Price	ثَـمَـن	47.	

LESSON 15

Dialogue 21: Inviting a Friend to A Movie

مصطفى	يا هِبَة، هَل تَذْهَبينَ مَعي إلى السِّـينِما هَذا المَساء؟
هبة	آسِفة يا مُصْطَفىَ، لَيْس هَذا المَساء، أنا مَشْغولة جِداً مَعَ أُمِّي وَ أَخي الصَّغير.
مصطفى	هَل هُناك مُناسَـبَـة؟
هبة	نـَعَم، اليَـوْم هُوَ عِـيـدُ مِـيلاد أَخي طارِق.
مصطفى	كَمْ سَـنـةً عُـمْـرُهُ؟
هبة:	عُـمْـرهُ خَـمْـسَة عَـشْرَة سَـنَـة.
مصطفى	كُـل عَام وِ هُوَ طَـيِّـب وَ بِـخَـيْـر.
هبة	و أنتَ دائِماً طَـيِّـب يا مصطفى.

Dialogue 21 Vocabulary

1) Busy/ occupied	مَشْغولة
2) Occasion	مُناسَـبَـة
3) His Age	عُـمْـرُهُ
4) Fine/ delicious / good	طَـيِّـب
5) Always	دائِماً

Activity 1: Invite your friend to a movie and plan to when you should meet. Get inspired by the previous dialogue and be creative.

Education التَّعْليم

Report Card			شَهادَة مَدْرَسِيَّة	
Final Grade	Second semester	First semester	اِسْم الطَّالب: أيْمن مُراد	
الدَّرجة النِّهائِيَّة	الفَتْرَة الثَّانِيَة	الفَتْرَة الأُولَى	Subject	المَادَة
			English language	اللُّغة الإنْجِليزيَّة
			French language	اللُّغة الفَرنسيَّة
			German language	اللُّغة الألْمانِيَّة
			Italian language	اللُّغة الإيطاليَّة
			Computer	حَاسُوب
			Mathematics	رِياضِيَّات
			Statistics	إحْصاء
			Chemistry	كِيمْياء
			Physics	فِيزْياء
			Algebra	الجَبْر
			Biology	الأَحْياء
			Geology	جِيُولوجْيا
			Discipline	سُلوك

Education Vocabulary List

1. **Second semester**	الفَتْرَة الثَّانِيَة	7) First semester	الفَتْرَة الأُولَى
2. **Chemistry**	كِيمْياء	8) Final Grade	الدَّرجة النّهائِيَّة
3. **Physics**	فِيزْياء	9) Statistics	إِحْصاء
4. **Algebra**	الجَبْر	10) Chemistry	كِيمْياء
5. **Biology**	الأَحْياء	11) Discipline	سُلوك
6. **Geology**	جِيُولوجْيا	12) Education	التَّعْليم

Activity 2: In a one paragraph, talk about your education, include the names of your high school, middle school and elementary school, include the subjects you liked and disliked.

Travel السَّـفَر

The Continents القارَّات

List the 6 continents				

خَريطَة الوِلايَات المُتَحِدَة الأمْريكِيّـة

List all the states you recognize on the map							
.8	.7	.6	.5	.4	.3	.2	.1
.16	.15	.14	.13	.12	.11	.10	.9
.24	.23	.22	.21	.20	.19	.18	.17
.32	.31	.30	.29	.28	.27	.26	.25
.40	.39	.38	.37	.36	.35	.34	.33
.48	.47	.46	.45	.44	.43	.42	.41

خَريطَة أمْريــكا الوُسْـــطــى

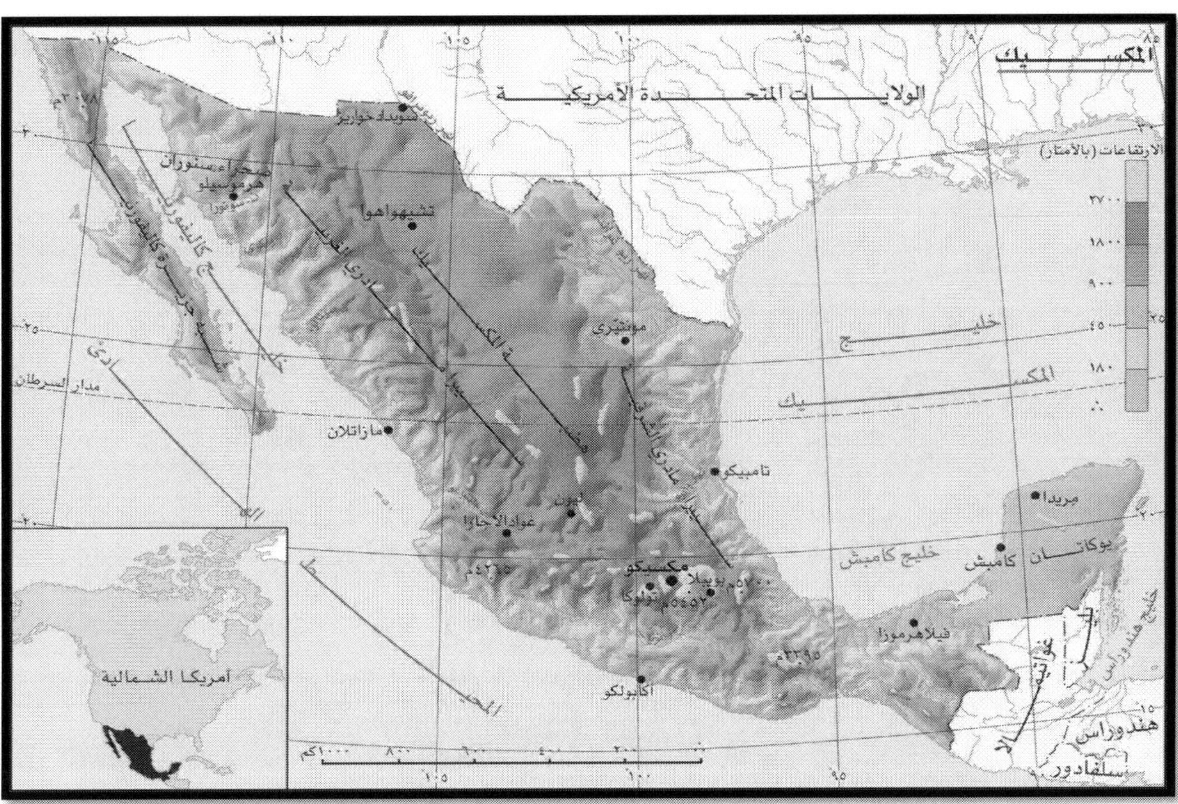

List all the countries you recognize on te map

خَريطة دُوَل أمْريكا الجَنوبِـيَّة

List all the countries you recognize on te map				
.5	.4	.3	.2	.1
.10	.9	.8	.7	.6
.15	.14	.13	.12	.11

خريطة دُوَل الجَامِعَــة العَــرَبية

List all the countries you recognize on the map and their English equivalent			
4.	3.	2.	1.
8.	7.	6.	5.
12.	11.	10.	9.
16.	15.	14.	13.
20.	19.	18.	17.

خريطة دُوَل أُوروبًّا و جُـزْء آسْيا

List all the countries that you recognize on the map or wish to visit.			
.4	.3	.2	**.1**
.8	.7	.6	.5
.12	.11	.10	.9
.16	.15	.14	.13
.20	.19	.18	.17
.24	.23	.22	.21
.28	.27	.26	.25
.32	.31	.30	.29

خريطة دول أفْريقيا

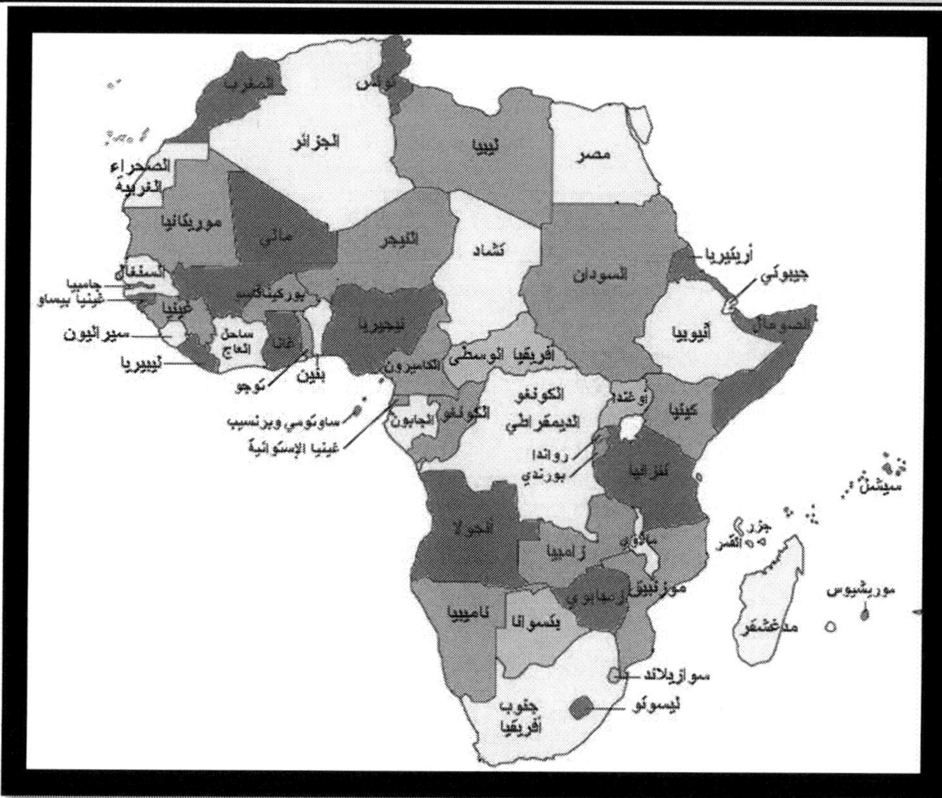

List all the countries that you recognize on the map or wish to visit.			
4.	3.	2.	1.
8.	7.	6.	5.
12.	11.	10.	9.
16.	15.	14.	13.
20.	19.	18.	17.
24.	23.	22.	21.
28.	27.	26.	25.

دُول قارَة آسيا

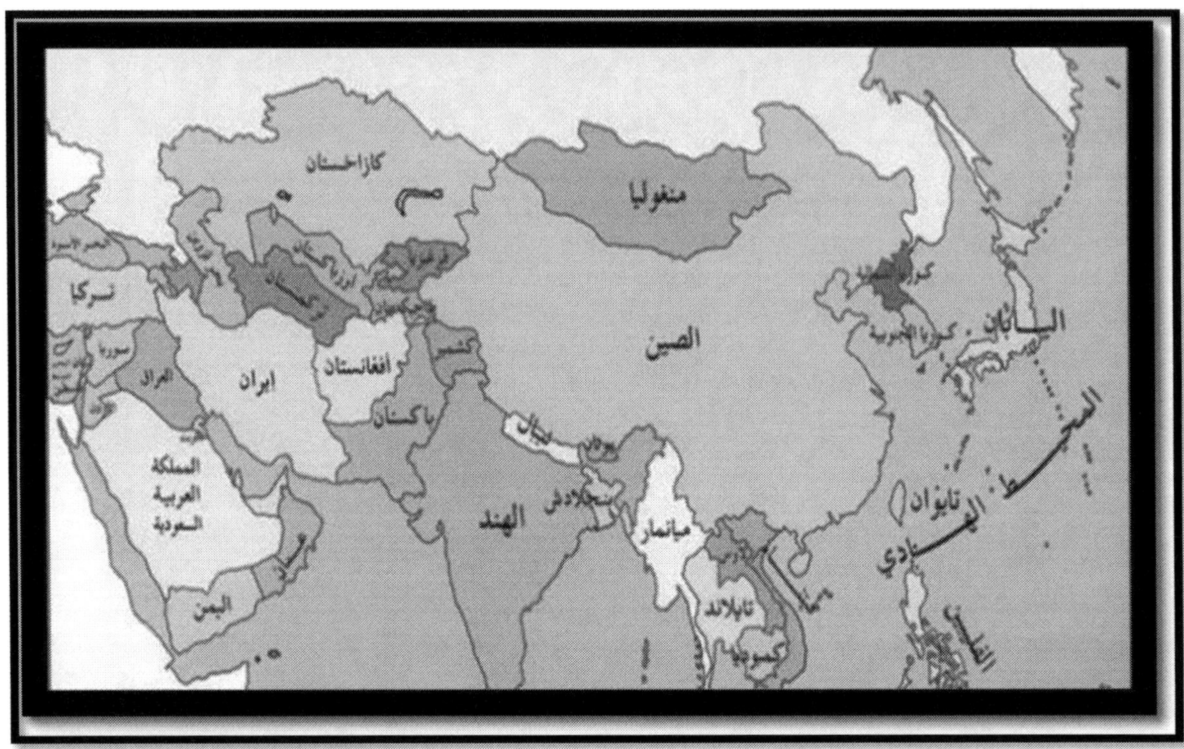

List all the countries that you recognize on the map or wish to visit.			
4.	3.	2.	1.
8.	7.	6.	5.
12.	11.	10.	9.
16.	15.	14.	13.
20.	19.	18.	17.

خريطة اللُّغات الإيرانية

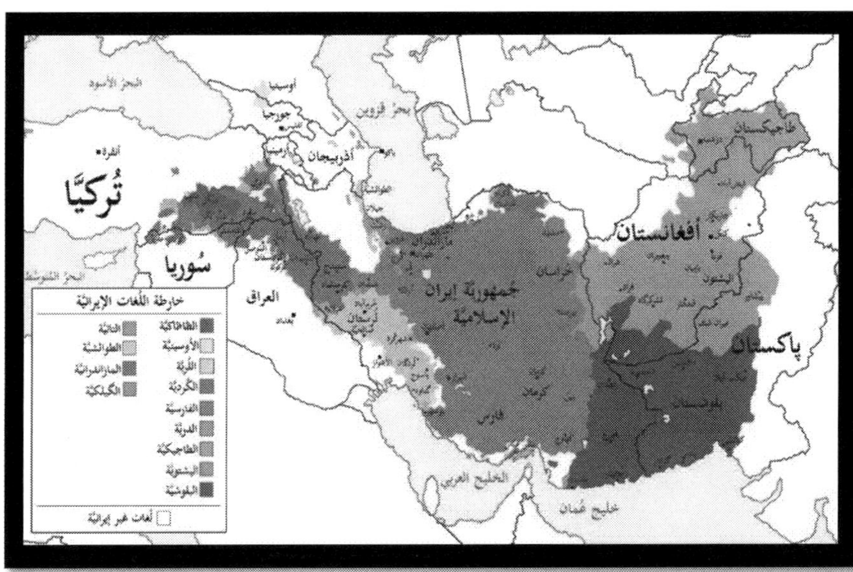

خريطة أستراليا و نيوزيلاندا

List all the countries that you recognize on the map or wish to visit.			
4.	3.	2.	1.
8.	7.	6.	5.

Dialogue 22: Geography Class in Cairo

الطالب	يا أستاذ، أيْـنَ تـقَع الوِلايات المُـتـَحِـدة الأَمْريكيَّة؟
الأستاذ	الوِلايات المُـتـحِدة الأمْريكية تَـقَع في قارَّة أمْريكا الشَّماليَّة
الطالب	يا أستاذ، أيْن تَـقَع دوْلَة الهِنْد؟
الأستاذ	دَوْلة الهِند تَقَع في قارة آسْيا
الطالب	يا أستاذ، أين تَقع دوْلة جَنوب أفْريقْيا؟
الأستاذ	دولة جَنوب أفْريقيا تَقع في قارة أفريقيا
الطالب	يا أستاذ، أيْن تَقَع دولة الـنِّـمْـسا؟
الأستاذ	دولة النِّـمْسا تَـقع في قارَّة أُوروبَّا

Dialogue 22 Vocabulary

2)	Continent	قارة	1)	To Fall / To be located	تقع / وقع
4)	Where	أين	3)	USA	الولايات المتحدة الأمريكية
6)	Austria	النمسا	5)	Country	دولة
8)	India	الهند	7)	Countries	دول

Activity 2: With your class partner, read the coined names of thee states listed in the table below and write the name of the state in the provided space:

	9. وِلايةُ المُحيط		1. الوِلايةُ الفِضِّيَّة
	10.ولاية البُرْتُقال		2. ولاية البَوابة الذَّهبِيَّة
	11.الوِلاية الخَضْراء دائِماً		3. الوِلاية الأُولى
	12.ولايـة الخُوخ		4. ولاية الجَبلِ الأَخْضَر
	13.وِلاية الوادي العَظيم		5. وِلاية العُشبِ الأزْرق
	14.ولاية الأحْجار الكَريمَة		6. ولاية الخَلج
	15.ولاية البُحيْرات العُظْمى		7. ولاية خليَّة النَّحْلِ
	16.وِلايةُ الأَرْضِ السَّاحِرَة		8. وِلايةُ النَّجْمَةِ الوَحِيدَة
		17. ولاية الشّمْسِ المُشْرِقَة	

Helping Vocabulary For Activity 2			
Grand Canyon	الوادي العَظيم	Mountain	الجَبلِ
Bay / Gulf	الخليج	Grass	العُشبِ
Gemstone	الأحجار الكريمة	Beehive	خلية النحل
Lakes	البحيرات	Lone/ Lonly	الوَحِيدَة
Land	الأَرْضِ	Enchantment / Magical	السَّاحِرَة

Activity 3: Your friend from the Middle East is visiting you in the united states. He handed you a list of landmarks in Arabic, read the list and identify them in English in the space provided

(I want to Visit)................. أُريدُ أنْ أزورَ			
	متحف المسميسونيون		البيت الأبيض
	جران كانيون		جولدن جيت
	ألكاتراز		إمباير إستيت
	تشاينا تون		هوليوود
	مكتبة الكونجرس		لاس فيجاس

Activity 4: With your class partner talk about your state and its coined name and the most important landmarks he / she might visit. Prepare your thoughts in the space provided:

Passage 2: Planning A Vacation

التَّخْطيط لِعُطْلَة

اسْمي نادِر، في عُطْلَة الصَّيْف، سأذْهبُ إلى مَدينة واشِنطن لِزيارة جَدِّي وَ جَدَّتي، وَ هُناك سَأزور مَتْحَف المِسمسونيان و البَيْت الأَبْيَض. في الأُسْبوعْ الثّاني مِنْ العُطْلة، سَأذهبُ إلى مَدينَة نِيويورك بالحافِلةْ و هُناك سأذْهبُ مَعَ صديقي جُون إلى تِمْثال الحُرية و مَبْنى الإمْبايَر إسْتيت. أَيْضاً سَنَذْهَبُ إلى مَسْرح بْرودواي في مَساءِ يَوْمِ السَّبْتْ الثَّاني و العِشْرين مِن شَهْر يُونيو. بَعْدَ ذَلِك، سَنَزور مَتْحَف المِتروبوليتان و حَديقَة الهايْد بارْك. في يَوْم ثلاثون من شهْر يُونيو سَنَعودُ إلى مَدينة واشِنْطون.

Passage 2 Vocabulary

Building	مَبْنى	Vacation	عُطْلَة
Theatre	مَسْرح	I will visit	سأزُور
After that	بَعْدَ ذَلِك	Museum	مَتْحف
We will visit	سَنزور	Statue	تِمْثال
We will visit	سَنعود	Freedom	الحُرِّيَّة

Activity 5: Answer the following questions in Arabic:

1)	Where will Nader go in the Summer vacation? -- -- -- -- -- --
2)	Who is accompanying Nader in his trip? -- -- -- -- -- --

3)	What city are they planning to visit?
4)	What are the landmarks they are planning on visiting?
5)	What is the mean of transportation mentioned in the passage?
6)	When will Nader return from his vacation?

Passage 3: New York City

مَـديـنَـةُ نـيـُويـورك

مَدينَةُ نُيويورك هِي أكْبَرُ مَدينةْ في الوِلاياتِ المُتَّحِدة الأمْريكيَّة.

أكْثَرَ مِن ثَمانِيَة مَلايـيـن شَخْصٍ يَعيشونَ فِيها.

أيْضاً، مَدينَةُ نِيويورك هِي مَقَرْ الأُمَمْ المُتَّحِدَة.

مَدينة نيويورك تَقَعُ في وِلايَةِ نيويورك. في مدينة نيويورك حَوالَيّ مِئتيْنِ

وخَمْسينِ مُتْحَفاً، و كَذَلِكَ شارِع بْرودْوَاي الشَّهير على مُسْتَوى

العَالَم بِالعُروض التَّرْفِيهيَّة.

مدينة نيويورك هِي عاصِمَةُ الأعْمال في العَالَمْ وَ بِها العَديدْ مِنْ الشَّرِكات

الدُوَلِيَّة و بُورْصَة نيويورك.

Passage 3 Vocabulary

2. Museum	مُتْحَفاً	1. The biggest	الأكْبَر
4. Street	شـارِع	3. The most	الأكْثَر
6. The famous	الشَّـهـير	5. Person	شَخْص
8. Level	مُسْتوى	7. They live	هُم يَعيشـون
10. World	العَالَم	9. Headquarter	مَقَر
12. With Shows	بـالعُروض	11. United Nations	الأُمَم المُـتَّـحِـدَة
14. Entertaining	التَّرْفِـيهـيـَّة	13. To locate/ to fall	تَقَع
16. Businesses	الأعْمال	15. Capital	عاصِمة
Companies	الشَّرِكات	Many	العَديد
Stock Market	بُـورْصَـة	international	الدُوَلِيَّـة

Activity 6: Fill in the blank. Use vocabulary from passage 2.

مدينة نيويورك هي .... مدينة في ولاية نيويورك
يعيش في نيويورك .... ملايين شخص
يقع متحف المتروبوليتان في ....
في نيويورك حوالي .... متحفاً
شارع برودواي مشهور بـــــ ....
مدينة نيويورك هي عاصمة الأعمال و فيها............... و ....

Activity 7: Passage 4: Jordan is writing and email to his Dad telling him about his daily activities. Write in English in the space provided what he does each day, in details:

أبي العزيز،

أكتب إليك من غرفتي في المدينة الجامعية، أنا أسكن مع زميلي چيمس في غرفة كبيرة في المبنى الشمالي. أذهب إلى المدرسة كل يوم في الصباح من الساعة السابعة إلى الساعة الثالثة عصراً. لا أذهب إلى الجامعة في يوم السبت و الأحد. في المساء في حوالي الساعة السادسة، أذهب إلى المركز الرياضي. أعود إلى غرفتي في الساعة السابعة، أدرس من الساعة السابعة و النصف إلى الساعة العاشرة مساء. في يوم السبت أذهب إلى السينما مع صديقتي سارة و في المساء أذهب إلى البقال و أشتري طعام الأسبوع.

أقضي يوم الأحد في الغرفة و أشاهد التلفاز و أنا آكل البيتزا.

Activity 8: Fill in the blank to complete the passage. Use the given word bank.

كبير	ريم	أرز	مدينة	الأربعاء	اسكن	أنام	العشاء
حوالي	خضراء	الجامعة	الجمعة	طبيبة	سنة	عطلة	الشتاء
أشاهد	الكيمياء	الصيف	بارد جداً	معي	الطقس	عشرون	تقع
	أستاذ	السادسة	الأسبوع	الكبير	الإسكندرية	مشوي	

أنا طالبة في .... و أدرس التاريخ. .... مع

صديقتي في غرفة كبيرة في بيت............... قديم في.............. القاهرة.

في فصل................. أذهب إلى الجامعة كل يوم، من الإثنين

إلى.................. بسيارتي و ....صديقتي.

سيارتي.................... ماركة هوندا موديل.............. الفين و

واحد . صديقتي اسمها ....و هي تدرس العلوم. ريم تريد أن

تكون..................

في المساء .... الخامسة ، نعود إلى البيت . في وجبة

.................نأكل دجاج................. و بطاطس و بروكلي في يوم الإثنين

ويوم................. في يوم الثلاثاء و يوم الخميس نأكل لحم

و............. و بروكلي أيضاً. أنا أحب البروكلي جداً.

أقضي .... نهاية ....مع أسرتي في

مدينة الإسكندرية. أسرتي صغيرة، أبي ....بالجامعة و أمي

مهندسة أما أخي.......... فهو يدرس

..........بجامعة الإسكندرية. أخي الصغير عمره

..........سنة و هو أيضاً يدرس الجغرافيا في

جامعة..........

..........الإسكندرية في شمال القاهرة.

..........هناك معتدل في فصل

..........و ....في فصل الشتاء. أعود إلي

بيتي في القاهرة يوم الأحد مساء في حوالي الساعة..........

أقضي مساء الأحد في غرفتي ، ....التلفاز ثم

..........في التاسعة.

ذَهَبَ

الضمائر	الماضي المعلوم	المضارع المعلوم	الأمر
أنا	ذَهَبْتُ	أَذْهَبُ	
أنت	ذَهَبْتَ	تَذْهَبُ	اِذْهَبْ
أنتِ	ذَهَبْتِ	تَذْهَبِينَ	اِذْهَبِي
هو	ذَهَبَ	يَذْهَبُ	
هي	ذَهَبَتْ	تَذْهَبُ	
أنتما	ذَهَبْتُمَا	تَذْهَبَانِ	اِذْهَبَا
أنتما مؤنث	ذَهَبْتُمَا	تَذْهَبَانِ	اِذْهَبَا
هما	ذَهَبَا	يَذْهَبَانِ	
هما مؤنث	ذَهَبَتَا	تَذْهَبَانِ	
نحن	ذَهَبْنَا	نَذْهَبُ	
أنتم	ذَهَبْتُم	تَذْهَبُونَ	اِذْهَبُوا
أنتن	ذَهَبْتُنَّ	تَذْهَبْنَ	اِذْهَبْنَ
هم	ذَهَبُوا	يَذْهَبُونَ	
هن	ذَهَبْنَ	يَذْهَبْنَ	

Lesson 15 Vocabulary List

1. **North**	شَمال	49. Compass	بوصلة
2. **South**	جَنوب	50. Distance	مسافة
3. **East**	شرق	51. Area	مساحة
4. **West**	غرب	52. Width	عرض
5. **Direction**	اتجاه	53. Height	ارتفاع
6. **Left**	يسار	54. Length	طول
7. **Right**	يمين	55. Place; Location	مكان / أماكن
8. **Behind**	وراء	56. Location, Site	موقع / مواقع
	خلف	57. Capital	عاصمة / عواصم
9. **In Front Of**	أمام	58. Suburb	ضاحية / ضواح
10. **Above**	فوق	59. The Country	الريف
11. **Below**	تحت	60. Village	قرى / قرية
12. **Map**	خريطة /خرائط	61. District	أحياء / حيّ
	خارطة	62. Governorate	محافظة
13. **Region, Area**	منطقة مناطق	63. Country	بلد / بلاد

14. **Region**	**إقليم أقاليم**	64. Homeland, Nation	**وطن / أوطان**
15. **North America**	**أمريكا الشمالية**	65. Europe	**أوروبا**
16. **South America**	**أمريكا الجنوبية**	66. Africa	**أفريقيا**
17. **The United States**	**الولايات المتحدة الأمريكية** **أمريكا**	67. Asia	**أسيا**
18. **Austria**	**النمسا**	68. Australia	**أستراليا**
19. **Venice**	**البندقية**	69. The United Kingdom	**المملكة المتحدة**
20. **Germany**	**ألمانيا**	70. England	**إنجلترا**
21. **Greece**	**اليونان**	71. The Middle East	**الشرق الأوسط**
22. **China**	**الصين**	72. Sudan	**السودان**
23. **Japan**	**اليابان**	73. Khartoum	**الخرطوم**
24. **India**	**الهند**	74. Morocco	**المغرب**
25. **North Africa**	**شمال أفريقيا**	75. Casablanca	**الدار البيضاء**
26. **The Maghreb (North Africa)**	**المغرب**	76. Marrakesh	**مراكش**
27. **The Mashriq (The Middle East)**	**المشرق**	77. Algeria	**الجزائر**
28. **Egypt**	**مصر**	78. Algiers	**الجزائر**
29. **Cairo**	**القاهرة**	79. Tunisia	**تونس**
30. **Alexandria**	**الإسكندرية**	80. Tunis	**تونس**

31. **Hurghada**	**الغردقة**	81. Libya	**ليبيا**
32. **Sharm Al-Sheikh**	**شرم الشيخ**	82. Tripoli	**طرابلس**
33. **Luxor**	**الأقصر**	83. Benghazi	**بنغازي**
34. **Aswan**	**أسوان**	84. Levant	**الشام**
35. **Sinai**	**سيناء**	85. Jordan	**الأردن**
36. **Upper Egypt**	**الصعيد**	86. Amman	**عمّان**
37. **Israel**	**إسرائيل**	87. Palestine	**فلسطين**
38. **Rabat**	**الرباط**	88. The West Bank	**الضفة الغربية**
39. **Sana'a**	**صنعاء**	89. Gaza Strip	**قطاع غزة**
40. **Doha**	**الدوحة**	90. Jerusalem	**القدس**
41. **Lebanon**	**لبنان**	91. Kuwait City	**مدينة الكويت**
42. **Beirut**	**بيروت**	92. Bahrain	**البحرين**
43. **Syria**	**سوريا**	93. Manama	**المنامة**
44. **Damascus**	**دمشق**	94. Saudi Arabia	**المملكة العربية السعودية**
45. **Iraq**	**العراق**	95. Riyadh	**الرياض**
46. **Baghdad**	**بغداد**	96. Mecca	**مكّة (المكرّمة)**
47. **Kuwait**	**الكويت**	97. Medina	**المدينة (المنوّرة)**

48. **United Arab Emirates**	**الإمارات العربية المتحدة**	98. Qatar	**قطر**
49. **The ocean**	**المحيط**	99. The gulf	**الخليج**
50. **The mountain**	**الجبل**	100. The river	**النهر**
51. **The island**	**الجزيرة**	101. The sea	**البحر**

* Note that countries and cities are usually feminine, except those specifically noted as masculine.

Practice Activities

Choose the proper word to complete the meaning of each sentence:

1) صديقتي .... (جميلة – جديد – زميل)

2) .... تحب مدينة " رينو"؟ (هل – أنا – ماذا)

3) هذا ابني .... (الصغير– القميص- الطاولة)

4) .... غداّ إلى سوريا) سأسافر – أحب أن- لا أحب)

5) إلى اللقاء في .... إن شاء الله (لبنان - طاولة – باب- شباك)

6) هذه .... لبنى (زوجتي – كتاب - كرسي- ليمون)

7) هذا ....ʺ جون ʺ (زميلي – كتابي- قلمي)

8) مكتبي .... السبورة (اكتب - قرب - أكلت)

9) .... البنت؟ (مَـــن- أكل- هذه -- مِـــن)

10) هناك علم ....(هذا – هذ - جديدة - كبير – هنا)

11) .... في الغُرفة ثلاجة صغيرة (هنا – بالقرب – هذا)

12) هناك .... كبير في الغرفة (تلفزيون – ماكينة قهوة – سجادة)

13) .... الحال ؟ (هل – ماذا – كيف)

14) .... اسمك ؟ (هل- ما – كيف)

15) .... صغير (العالم – ربما – أكتب – عند)

16) .... أبي و أمي (أمشي - أقضي – أحب)

17) .... سيارة جديدة (معي - قرب - عن)

18) .... أَين أنتِ ؟ (متى – مِن – مَن - أنتَ)

19) المُعلم .... الباب (قرب - هناك - ربما)

20) .... معكِ دولار ؟ (أين - هل - ماذا - متى)

21) اسمي آدم ، و .... اسمك ؟ (ماذا – ما - متى)

22) هَذه هي .... الجديدة (الأستاذ - المعلمة - القلم)

23) الأُستاذة الجَديدة من .... (سيارة - إفريقية - قلم - هناك)

24) " جون " من أمريكا ، هو .... (برتغالية - لبناني - أمريكي)

25) July، هو .... (يوليو - يونيو - يناير)

26) .... في مدينة " رينو" (أسكن - ألعب - أدرس)

27) .... من وِلاية " تكساس" (أسرتي - سلة - كرة)

28) يا " سلامة ، .... تَفْعل هنا ؟ (من – ماذا – متى)

29) .... الكُرة مَع صَديقي (أدرس- ألعب - أسكن)

30) مَدينة "ساكرامنتو" .... عن هنا (بعيدة - قريب - ممتاز)

31) حنان................. (لبناني- سوري - لبنانية)

32) أهلا يا منى ، .... (ممتاز - تشرفنا - هناك)

33) .... سَعيدة (أسعد - قرب - فرصة)

34) أنا .... في .... (أسكن - مطعم - أدرس - أعمل – بيت)

35) أبي............. و أُمي .... (نادي – مهندس - أستاذة – ربما)

36) .... المَدْرسة كبيرة (جامعة - كرة - حافلة)

37) .... الصف كبير (ملعب - جامعة - شباك)

38) بيت.......... كبير (جدتي – المدرسة - الجامعة - القلم)

39) هذه مدينة .... (قديمة - ممتاز – كبير – هنا)

40) أنا......... الموسيقى (أسكن - أحب - قرب - من أين)

41) .... صباحا، تسافر معي (هناك - غداً - ممتاز)

42) إلى .... في كاليفورنيا مساءً (من - لماذا - هل - اللقاء)

43) يا أمي، شكرا على .... (كل شيء - ممتاز - أبي - لا أحب)

44) مع .... يا أمي (اسمي - السلامة - السيارة)

45) أنا أعرف .... (هناك - ممتاز - عندي - الجواب)

46) .... العربية جميلة (اللغة - ضابط - طيار – أمريكي)

47) أخي .... في القوات الجوية (بيت - غسالة - طيَّار)

48) .... كبيرة و عندي .... جديد (غرفتي - ممتاز - جديدة – زوجي)

49) .... عطلة عيد الميلاد في البيت (أدرس - اقضي - ألعب)

50) أحب .... في الصباح (القهوة - الكرة - الثلاجة)

51) زميلتي .... (جميلة – جديد – زميل)

52) .... تحب مدينة " سان فرانسيسكو"؟ (هل – أنا – ماذا)

53) هذه ابنتي .... (الصغيرة– القمري- الطاولة)

54) .... غداً إلى "نيويورك" (سأسافر – أحب - لا أحب)

55) إلى .... في " لوس أنجلوس"، .... (إن شاء الله - اللقاء – شباك)

56) هذه .... سلمى (زوجتي - كرسي- ليمون)

57) هذا ...."جون" (صديقي – كتابي- قلمي)

58) طاولتي................ السبورة (اكتب - قرب - أكلت)

59) .... // .... الولد؟ (مَــن - هذا - مِــن)

60) هناك علم ....(هذا - قديمة - كبير – هنا)

61) هنا في .... ثلاجة صغيرة (بالقرب – الغُرفة - هذا)

62) هناك .... قديمة في الغرفة (تلفزيون – ماكينة قهوة – قلم)

63) .... حالكَ ؟ (هل – ماذا – كيف)

64) .... صغير (العالم – أكتب – حنان)

65) .... أبي و أمي (أمشي - أقضي – أحب)

66) .... سيارة جديدة (معي - أقضي - عن)

67) .... أَين أنتِ ؟ (متى – مِن - مَن)

68) هَذه هي .... الجديدة (العلم - المعلمة - القلم)

69) الأُستاذة الجَديدة من .... (سيارة - إفريقية - هناك)

70) " چون " من أمريكا ، هو .... (برتغالية - لبناني - أمريكيّ)

71) June، هو .... (يوليو - يونيو - يناير)

72) .... في مدينة " سباركس" (أسكن - بعيدة - أدرس)

73) .... مِن وِلاية " نبراسكا " (أسرتي - ماذا - كرة)

74) يا " سلامة ، .... تَفْعل هنا ؟ (أين – ماذا – متى)

75) .... الكُرة مَع صَديقي (السلة- ألعب - أفعل)

76) مَدينة "سانتا بربرا" .... عن هنا (بعيدة - قريب - ممتازة)

77) "سوزان" .... (لبناني- سوري - لبنانية)

78) أهلا يا "چولـيا" ، .... (ممتاز - تشرفنا - هناك)

79) .... سَعيدة، يا حنان. (أسعد - قرب - فرصة)

80) أنا .... في .... (أسكن - مطعم - أدرس - أعمل)

81) أبي.................. و أُمي .... (نادي – مهندسة - أستاذ)

82) .... المَدْرسة كبيرة (مكتب - كرة - حافلة)

83) .... الصَّف كبيــــر (سيارة - جامعة - شُباك)

84) في بيت جدتي .... جميل (أثاث - الجامعة - سبورة)

85) هذه مدينة .... (قديمة - ممتاز – كبير)

86) أنا.................. الموسيقى (أسكن - أحب - من أين)

87) .... صباحاً، تســـــافر معــــي. (هناك - غداً - ممتاز)

88) إلى .... في " سان دييجو" ، مساءً. (لماذا - هل - اللقاء)

89) يا أمــــــي، شكراّ على .... (كل شيء - ممتاز - لا أحب)

90) مع .... يا أمي. (اللغة - السلامة - السيارة)

91) أنا أعرف .... (عندي - الجواب - ممتاز)

92) .... العربية جميلة (اللغة - ضابط - فرنسا)

93) غرفتي .... و عندي .... جديد (كبيرة - ممتاز – مايكروويف)

94) .... عطلة عيد ....في بيت أسرتي (الميلاد - اقضي - ألعب)

95) أحب .... في الصباح (القهوة - الميلاد - الجوية)

96) الساعة الرابعة و خمس .... (دقيقة - دقائق - ساعات)

Fill in the blank using the given words in the table below:

الكبير	أستاذ	العشاء	أنام	اسكن	الأربعاء	مدينة	أرز	ريم	كبير
مشوي	طبيبة	الشتاء	عطلة	سنة	الأسبوع	الجمعة	الجامعة	خضراء	حوالي
معي	أشاهد	تقع	عشرون	الطقس	الإسكندرية	بارد جدا	الصيف	الكيمياء	السادسة

أنا طالبة في ....و أدرس التاريخ.   .... مع صديقتي في غرفة كبيرة في بيت.............. قديم

في.............. القاهرة. في فصل.............. أذهب إلى الجامعة كل يوم، من الإثنين إلى..............

بسيارتي و .... صديقتي. سيارتي.............. ماركة هوندا موديل.............. ألفيين و

واحد. صديقتي اسمها .... و هي تدرس العلوم. ريم تريد أن تكون..............

في المساء ....الخامسة ، نعود إلى البيت . في وجبة ....نأكل دجاج.............. و بطاطس و بروكلي

في يوم الإثنين و يوم.............. .

في يوم الثلاثاء و يوم الخميس نأكل لحم و.............. و بروكلي أيضاَ. أنا أحب البروكلي جداَ.

أقضي .... نهاية..............مع أسرتي في مدينة الإسكندرية. أسرتي صغيرة، أبي

..............بالجامعة و أمي مهندسة أما أخي.............. فهو يدرس

..............بجامعة الإسكندرية. أخي الصغير عمره ....سنة و هو أيضاَ يدرس الجغرافيا

في جامعة..............

..............الإسكندرية في شمال القاهرة. ....هناك معتدل في فصل

.... و ....في فصل الشتاء. أعود إلي بيتي في القاهرة يوم الأحد مساء في حوالي

الساعة..............

أقضي مساء الأحد في غرفتي، ....التلفاز ثم ....في التاسعة.

ABOUT THE AUTHOR

Dahlia Dwedar, *PhD*
Curriculum and Instruction
Education Technology Management
Art and Literature Criticism
DDWEDAR@UNR.EDU

Program Committee Chair
Of The
Arabic language & Middle Eastern Cultures
2013- Present

University of Nevada, Reno |
College of Liberal Arts
Department of World languages & literatures

Made in the USA
San Bernardino, CA
14 August 2020